Transformed

GRAND-DAD'S STORY

CAMERON D. ARMSTRONG

RELIANT PUBLISHING
A DIVISION OF REDEMPTION PRESS

Published by Reliant Publishing, an imprint of Redemption Press, PO Box 427, Enumclaw, WA 98022.

Toll-Free (844) 2REDEEM (273-3336)

Redemption Press is honored to present this title in partnership with the author. The views expressed or implied in this work are those of the author. Redemption Press provides our imprint seal representing design excellence, creative content, and high quality production.

ISBN 13: 978-1-64645-392-4

Library of Congress Catalog Card Number: 2021902043

To the family of Buford C. "Buzz" Armstrong

This is our story.

Table of Contents

Introduction

The first and last time my daughter met my Grand-Dad was in a hospital room. She was sixteen months old and jet-lagged. On February 1, 2018, our plane crossed the Atlantic Ocean and landed in Atlanta. Eleven days later, we boarded another plane bound for Muskegon, Michigan. Since he'd spent months in and out of the hospital, my wife and I knew this could be our only chance for Grand-Dad to meet Sara. We were right.

As my aunt Veronica and Grandmama ushered us into the hospital room, Grand-Dad was just emerging from surgery. His eyes should have remained distant. Instead they lit up with recognition as Grandmama told him he had visitors. For the next few hours, I introduced Grand-Dad to my daughter, Sara, and he astonished us all by asking questions about our life as missionaries in Romania. But that was not the most extraordinary thing I remember.

News in the form of a phone call told us that one of my many cousins was hurt and needed prayer. This was nothing new to me, considering I have twenty-five first cousins. What was extraordinary was that Grand-Dad held out his hands for us to hold. Then he prayed. His deep, soothing, "Our heavenly Father . . ." is something I will always hear when I think of my Grand-Dad. From his hospital bed, Grand-Dad prayed. We all verbalized our amens. My daughter silently watched him. Less than two months later, Grand-Dad was gone.

My voice quivered as I asked Grandmama if I might deliver his memorial sermon, which I did on April 9, 2018. That manuscript is offered as an epilogue at the end of this biography. It was one of the quickest sermons I've ever prepared, if not *the* quickest, probably because I have reams of mental images of Grand-Dad. At least, I thought I did.

During the week of Valentine's Day 2020, precisely two years after we visited my Grand-Dad in the hospital, Aunt Veronica interviewed Grandmama for a church event concerning her love story with Grand-Dad. Thankfully, this interview was recorded on Facebook. From my balcony in Bucharest, Romania, I listened as Grandmama shared. I am not ashamed to say I wept. I wept for the legacy of Christ-honoring compassion left for us and then came to a realization. *Someone needs to write this down.*

My dad, whom I call by his nickname "Buzzie" in subsequent pages, taught me to use my gifts, accept challenges as they come, and see things through to the end. I suspect he learned that from his dad. So I accepted my own challenge. If someone needs to write this story, maybe it should be me. I then proposed the idea to my parents, who I'm pretty sure thought I was a bit off my rocker, and then to Grandmama, who graciously agreed to work with me.

This biography is composed of content taken from multiple interviews of family members. Academically speaking, the book could be called an exercise in oral history, since I am mostly weaving together spoken memories into a cohesive story. The rest of the details can be found, amazingly, in the public domain of the internet. When I needed to check facts, such as street locations, I simply *googled* them from my desk in Bucharest. For example, I watched a YouTube video of a car ride through Norwayne, Michigan, where Grand-Dad grew up.

For giving me a chance to interview and gather their memories, which I recorded and transcribed, I'd like to thank my Grand-Dad's sisters, Clara and Janet; Grand-Dad's nephew, Chuck; Grandmama Gayle's brothers, Em and Rich; my grandparents' children, Calvin (Buzzie), Daran, Valorie, Veronica, and Brooks; my brother, Conner; and my cousins, Brock, April, Amara, Grace, and Brayden.

For about six months, nearly every Thursday morning, which is evening in Romania, Grandmama and I spent hours over the phone interviewing, checking, and rechecking each chapter as I drafted them. I cannot thank her enough for her courage to allow this story to be printed, her love for all of us whose names dot these pages, and her prayers for God to be honored through this book's success. Thank you to my sister Kendall and Aunt Kelly for their thorough and thoughtful edits. And thanks goes to my lovely wife for valiantly keeping our two active, little children at bay during these times and for always putting up with my writing projects.

Working primarily from memory presents the danger that negative details will be either left out or altered. As much as possible, I have tried to present Grand-Dad as he was, faults and all, through the eyes of his loved ones. I hope that becomes clear from the start. My prayer from the outset is that the writing of Grand-Dad's story results in three things. First, I pray that family members like myself who only knew pieces of this story will be proud of the legacy of faith Grand-Dad has left us. Second, I pray that the Christian reader's faith is strengthened. Third, I pray that readers who are not Christians find themselves drawing nearer to the God of Buzz Armstrong as they read of his transformation.

Grand-Dad's story is uniquely familiar. It is unique because he lived a unique life. It is familiar because all of us who have encountered Jesus and responded in faith to his call experience transformation. In this sense, Grand-Dad's story echoes in the story of every Christian believer. May it also be the case for readers of this biography.

Soli Deo gloria—To God alone be the glory,

Cameron D. Armstrong
Bucharest, Romania
December 2020

CHAPTER 1

Rebel Without a Cause

"Do you think I have a good personality?" asked twelve-year-old Buford sheepishly.

"My goodness, you have a great personality! And a great smile!"

Buford had always liked the boarders, often from Tennessee, who paid to live in their spare room, eat meals at their dinner table, and work in the Detroit metro area. These men were treated as part of the family—like big brothers. But Buford especially liked Scotty, the man to whom he posed this quite personal question, believing he could confide in him. This particular affirmation gave Buford a great deal of confidence. He would recall that conversation for the rest of his life.

Nineteen miles east of Murfreesboro, Tennessee, sits the town of Woodbury, home to the Moonlite Drive-In Theater and county seat of Cannon County. Heading south on Tennessee State Route 53, take a slight right onto Sheyboygan Road and follow it for eighteen miles. Bouncing and curving will eventually bring you to the sleepy community of Hollow Springs, where a quick jaunt up Dickens Hill Road will bring you abruptly to an intersection at Gilley Hill Road. It is down Gilley Hill Road where Buford Armstrong's story begins. For down that road, a little, white Methodist church still stands proudly, and further down is the property once farmed by the Armstrong family, called The Ridge.

Born the sixth of eight children, Buford loved his parents fiercely. His father, John Hall Armstrong, was born on November 3, 1898. The product of a broken home, John vowed never to take his family for granted. John's mother appears to have been part Native American, perhaps named Roxanne, although it is impossible to know for sure how high or low was the actual genetic makeup.

John married Hessie Pearl Stacey, a local girl six years younger. Several Staceys are buried in the cemetery at the Gilley Hill Methodist Church, and so it seems they were one of the larger families in the area. Hessie could not have been more than twenty years old by the time she gave birth to her firstborn, Glyn, in 1924. Hessie always declared that she had married the "handsomest man in the county," which was a healthy sentiment considering she'd be bearing his children for the next twenty-one years. All but one of John and Hessie Armstrong's children were born in Tennessee: Glyn (b. 1924); John Jr., nicknamed Jack (b. 1927); Ruth (b. 1929); Clara (b. 1933); James (b. 1935); Buford (b. 1937); and Daryl (born January 12, 1940, and died January 16, 1940). Janet was the only child born in Michigan, and she was born soon after their arrival in Wayne, Michigan, in 1945.

Later in his life, Buford would always recollect fondly of his first eight years growing up in Tennessee. He was born on November 25, 1937, which was Thanksgiving Day. While Hessie had named all the other children, she evidently allowed John to have the final say in child number six. Two of John's friends were named Calvin and Buford, and thus the boy was christened Calvin Buford Armstrong. The problem was that Hessie did not care for the man named Calvin. So she called her son Buford. Into adulthood, he would introduce himself as Buford and even signed for his first Social Security card as "Buford C. Armstrong."

It was up to his mother to personally go and register his birth in Woodbury. Perhaps because Woodbury was quite a distance away when driving a horse and wagon or, more likely, because Hessie was exhausted, Buford was not registered until a few weeks later. Oddly, the clerk wrote November 15 on his birth certificate, so that became the day the family celebrated his birthday. Gayle, Buford's future wife, would later learn of this confusion and ask Hessie if they could begin celebrating on November 25. So, with Hessie's blessing, Buford began celebrating his birthday on the actual date of his birth.

Although farm life was difficult, there was a sense of constancy that gave life meaning. John did not own the land; he farmed it as a sharecropper, and the majority of the proceeds went to the farmer who owned the property. Sunday was for walking the mile or so to the Gilley Hill Methodist Church, often followed by a picnic lunch on the grounds. All the other days called for early mornings, when Buford's mother would wake him up and he would lug an enormous jug of water out to his father. By that point, his father would have been plowing sideways along their hillside farm for several hours. One morning Buford found his father struggling to get the horse moving. With steel in his eyes and fingers clenched, John punched the horse square between the eyes, causing the horse to buckle. "He never had a problem with that horse again," Buford would chuckle nostalgically.

Buford's constant playmate was his older brother James. Under the watchful eye of their sister Clara, Buford and James either invented games, like climbing ropes out of their barn's hay loft, or enjoyed more classic pleasures, like playing fetch with their dog Rover or playing a game of *hoop rolling*. In hoop rolling, children use a stick to roll a large, often wooden, hoop along the ground as long as possible before the hoop clatters to the ground. Recalled his future wife, Gayle, "He could keep that wheel rolling for the longest time and be running behind it. He said that for some reason it was a real challenge to see how long you could keep that going." Buford and James always played together, yet Clara was told to watch Buford a bit closer, since he was the more mischievous and riskier of the two.

Moonshine

Unfortunately, farming and selling cows' milk could not pay the bills. John knew there was another local answer to making quick money. He and some friends built a moonshine still in the woods nearby, selling the spirits to neighbors. Besides being illegal, distilling moonshine on your own is no easy task. If the proper concentrations are not met and if safety precautions are not taken, drinking the distilled spirits could result in kidney damage, blindness, or even death. During Prohibition many moonshiners used automotive radiators as condensers, often resulting in lead poisoning and blindness.

It is not clear the kinds of materials John or his friends used for their still. What is clear is that they were caught and sent to jail. A neighbor decided to report John to the police. Nowadays moonshiners can go to prison for up to five years. John spent thirty days in jail.

Upon John's release, Gilley Hill Methodist Church no longer welcomed the Armstrong family to their gatherings, effectively excommunicating them. The wound struck deep. "I'll never darken the door of another church," John vowed. It was a vow he would keep until his son Buford became a Christian.

In the middle of such turmoil, Buford's oldest brother, Glyn, returned home from the Navy. Now a veteran who had seen the economic prosperity of the northern states, Glyn urged his father and mother to pack up and move north. John had several relatives and friends in Wayne, Michigan, who assured him they could land him a quick job. So, with heavy hearts and the front yard full of their possessions for auction, the family turned their eyes north to Wayne, Michigan. Buford's sister Clara recalls boarding a train from Nashville and crying the whole ride north.

The Scrapper of Norwayne

On a sunny day in April 1945, the family arrived at the train station in Wayne. Relatives and friends housed the family temporarily. John went to work the very next day as an orderly at the Wayne County General Hospital, also called Eloise, where his relatives also worked. He continued to work there as an orderly, supervising male psychiatric patients, until his retirement in 1963.

Unfortunately, John finding immediate employment left Hessie to do the house hunting herself. Clara recalls their mother walking a mile in the rain each morning and evening to the housing office of the recently built neighborhood of Norwayne. Built in 1942 for defense workers and servicemen returning from the war, Norwayne was one of Detroit's early suburban neighborhoods. Clara remembered the scene well:

> Every day my mom would walk to the housing department in Norwayne. And she'd sit there in the housing department from 8:00 in the morning till 5:00 at night. She started on Monday, and they told her, "Well, you can just stay home. We'll call you when we have an opening."
> She said, "Well, that's okay. I'll just sit here and wait. Just in case you have something come up." She'd sit there and she'd read the paper. They told her all week, "We don't have an opening." But on Friday, they handed her the keys to a three-bedroom apartment. They said, "You deserve it. Here you go."

For John and the kids, the apartment, which was actually a duplex, was like a dream come true: large, close to town, and lots of young families with children. The community also boasted a neighborhood pool and several fields where kids could play baseball and football. "You could just step outside and get a ball game together and play with other kids," Buford recalled.

Yet the games were not always cordial. Hessie would often dress Buford in bright colors, usually red, so she could look out the window and pick him out of the crowd. More often than not, someone would issue a challenge and, while James would back down, Buford would step forward with fists raised. If it looked like the boy in red was about to get into another scrap, Hessie was prepared to break up the fistfight.

Because the duplex in Norwayne had a large upstairs with an extra room, the family took in single men as boarders. The extra money helped pay for a standard of living significantly higher than their Tennessee farm had allowed.

One boarder, nicknamed Pump Handle, had followed Ruth to Michigan after she graduated from high school in Woodbury, Tennessee. Not long after Pump Handle arrived, Ruth announced to him that she was in love with a Michigander named Bob Fox, whom she would later marry. Pump Handle took the news hard. Drinking heavily one night, Pump Handle awoke the next morning with a terrible hangover. Wanting some tomato juice to help him sober up, he placed a five-dollar bill in eight-year-old Buford's hand and asked him to take his wagon and go buy a large can of tomato juice. "Now I want you to be sure and get the tomato juice," said Pump Handle.

Buford set off, parked his wagon, entered the store, and immediately saw an enormous display of juicy pears. Gayle laughed as she related the story she'd heard from Buford:

> He bought five dollars' worth! They were his favorite fruit! So he thought, *Pump Handle is going to love these pears!* And he came home and the man was out on the yard looking down toward him and watching him come up.
>
> And when he got close, he said, "Where's my tomato juice?" Because he saw the bags.
>
> So [Buford] said, "Well, I figured you'd really like these pears."
> And the man said, "Oh, Lord have mercy!"

It is safe to say that young Buford had a mind of his own. Whether scrapping with other boys on the playing field or beaming with pride as he towed the world's best pears in his wagon, Buford was becoming a boy people remembered and usually liked being around. It was a personality trait that would mark him all his days.

Buzz

Although the family liked Norwayne well enough, Hessie longed for a house of their own. John's job at the hospital was not an easy one, but it did allow John and Hessie to save enough money for a down payment on a house. In 1951, about the time Buford turned thirteen, the family moved to a quaint house on Winifred Street, just across Michigan Avenue and across from the hospital where John worked. The Armstrongs set to work making their new house a home, and it would be home for about the next thirty years. Buford and the other kids quickly learned their way around the new neighborhood, making new friends and finding new ways to pass the time. The boarders still came and went, including the one who would tell Buford, "My goodness, you have a great personality!"

Unfortunately, a great personality is not the same as a clean record. Buford quickly became known among his new friends as a partier and troublemaker. They did not consider him a mean person; he had a magnetic personality, but he was definitely part of the rough-around-the-edges crowd. According to Gayle, Buford had a "penchant for finding trouble." He also loved joking around and making others laugh, even if the only one laughing was himself. One day in the lunch line, a girl had had enough of his joking, so she knocked the glass milk bottle he'd just received out of his hand and chipped his tooth. Buford's chipped tooth, which he would have the rest of his life, never darkened his grin.

Buford's junior high and high school years in Wayne were far more social than academic, which resulted in him failing the eleventh grade. Buford did enjoy a few subjects though, including Shakespearean dramas. He astonished everyone in school with his perfect recitation of a Hamlet soliloquy. Everyone at Wayne Memorial High School simply expected the usual cutup.

Early in his high school years, Buford's friends jokingly changed "Buford" to "Buzzard." But neither Buford nor his friends liked the sound of the word, so instead they shortened it to "Buzz." The nickname stuck. For the rest of his life, friends and family all called him "Buzz." (Since Buford assumed this nickname as his preferred name, always introducing himself as "Buzz," this moniker will be used for the remainder of the book.)

Running with the rough crowd also entailed darker hobbies, such as drinking heavily at parties, scrapping with teenage boys from nearby Inkster (with a knife scar on his back to prove it), and even spending some time in jail. Buzz's first jail-cell experience paradoxically involved encyclopedias. A local man hired Buzz and several of his friends to ride with him to Howell, Michigan, to sell encyclopedias door-to-door. The police were called when it was discovered they were all soliciting without a license, which ended in a one-night stay in the county jail. There were other incidents, too, but mostly all due to neighbors calling the police about the loud and obnoxious teenagers partying next door. Once the police became so annoyed with the teenagers that they cranked the heat in the cell just to teach them a lesson. Rarely did Buzz ever resist or talk back to the cops. But his friends would. On several occasions, Buzz saw his friends experience the business end of a nightstick.

One other life-or-death story that Buzz would vividly recall his whole life was when he and a buddy were speeding back to Wayne from Inkster. Buzz pleaded, "Please, you're gonna get us both killed." The friend, who clearly was intoxicated, had a "foot glued like lead to the floor," to quote the rock-n-roll song "Hot Rod Lincoln." Yet the police knew where they were going, so they set a roadblock in Buzz's neighborhood. When the car finally stopped, Buzz was allowed to go home. As Buzz looked back, he saw his friend yelling and trying to resist arrest as the nightsticks flew.

James Dean

As can be imagined, Buzz's extracurricular exploits earned him a reputation among other teens as a risk-taking cutup. Nevertheless, Buzz got along well with everyone and had lots of friends. He also had several girlfriends, whom he would take home to Winifred Street to meet his large family. Buzz's younger sister, Janet, remembers Buzz bringing them around all the time.

The hotspot for Wayne's teenagers was the local recreation center, which in the 1950s was open nearly every night. It was there that Buzz could display his ping-pong prowess and, once a week, kick off his shoes at the sock hop and twist the night away. Buzz made his way there as often as he could and dressed up for the weekly occasion.

Twenty years later, a Wayne police officer would pull over a car driven by Buzz and Gayle's second son, Daran. "Are you Buzz Armstrong's son?" Daran answered politely and affirmatively. The policeman then told Daran, "Well I want to tell you what he did when he'd come to that rec center." The officer had evidently been on duty when a teenage Buzz would come strolling through the doors like James Dean in *Rebel Without a Cause*. He relayed that Buzz's habit was to step into the door frame, lean one arm up onto the jamb, and simply look around to see who all was there. "It was like he was king of the mountain; it was just his place," Gayle said in between laughs.

Buzz believed high school was for making memories of life lived to the fullest. The past or future were not much on Buzz's mind. Yet all that changed one night when Buzz, now nineteen years old, glanced at the car next to his and saw the most beautiful teenage girl he'd ever seen sitting in the passenger seat.

CHAPTER 2

From Whence Cometh My Help?

Not many people remember their first personal prayers. "Lord, you can help me do this," prayed a five-year-old girl named Gayle. The problem was that even if the Lord believed that she could thread a needle, Gayle's mother wasn't so sure. Yet thread the needle she did, and Gayle considered that incident her first answered prayer. Thus began a prayer life that would change the destinies of countless individuals.

Buzz Armstrong's helpmate, Gayle, entered the world during one of the most turbulent months in United States history. On the morning of December 7, 1941, 353 Japanese fighter planes descended on the US naval base at Pearl Harbor, Hawaii, drawing the neutral United States into World War II. As the government scrambled to recruit soldiers and shift the population into war mode, a heavily pregnant woman named Georgina Cummins huddled over her radio and worried what the world might look like for her soon-to-arrive child. Less than three weeks later, on Christmas Eve Georgina gave birth to Gayle at Grace Hospital in downtown Detroit, Michigan. The nurses walked the hospital halls, smiling and singing Christmas carols.

Due to holding a job that was considered essential to the war effort, Gayle's father, Emery John Cummins, was exempt from becoming a soldier. A longtime employee of Ford Motor Company in Dearborn, Emery worked at Ford's Rouge plant, manufacturing airplanes for the war. By the time of Gayle's birth, Emery no longer labored on the assembly line but was a junior manager on his way up.

Georgina was a stay-at-home housewife. Yet that was only after their first child, Emery John Cummins II, was born. When Georgina married Emery in 1933, she was working for a telephone company in Detroit. Interestingly, national policy during the Great Depression dictated that married women could not hold jobs so as not to take away the jobs of the married, breadwinner men. In order to maintain the much-needed second income, from 1933 until 1937 Georgina neither wore a wedding ring nor informed her colleagues at the telephone company that she was married. After their first child was born, Georgina would never again work outside the home.

"A Real Happy Home"

Gayle grew up the middle child. Her older brother, Emery John (Em), nearly five years older, was evidently quite mischievous. Gayle recalled:

> For instance, I must have been three or four when he washed my face with snow for the first time. Right about that age. He was a rascal! And oh, did that hurt! I didn't realize it was going to hurt like it did. Of course, he surprised me too.

Yet Em cherished his little sister, always looking back fondly at the years he walked her from their brick house on Kendal Street in East Dearborn to William Ford Elementary School, a journey of several blocks.

Before Gayle started kindergarten, her brother Rich was born. With only two and a half years' difference, Gayle and Rich became dear playmates. Together they would hunt for insects, play on the playground, and reenact cowboy scenes from *Howdy Doody* and *Roy Rogers* they'd seen on the family's black-and-white television.

One telling example of Gayle as a child is of her love for their adopted cocker spaniel, who was far from kind and playful. "Now that dog was a mean dog," Em said. "That dog bit people! We had this little pet that bit people and hurt them. But my sis just had a soft spot in her heart for animals." When Gayle's parents finally gave the dog away, Gayle wept. Such a deep love for animals became a hallmark of Gayle's life.

A second example of Gayle's childhood comes from a first-grade Sunday school classroom. Through flannelgraph, the children learned Bible stories, important biblical truths, and the gospel. Although six-year-old Gayle had heard all her life that Jesus lived a sinless life, died on the cross for our sins, and rose again on the third day, she became convicted of her sin and need for a Savior. Reminiscing of the moment she became a Christian, Gayle said:

> It seems like maybe [the teacher] did the bridge from earth to heaven, with the cross being the bridge. Explaining that that's the only way to find Jesus. Yes, it was neat. A little bit about hell. They explained just a little. In order to go to heaven, you really needed to ask Jesus into your heart. I remember coming home and telling my mother and dad that I did need to do that, and I wanted to. So then they sat down with me and then we prayed together on our knees so that I could ask Jesus into my heart. It was sweet, you know. Real clear memory.

In 1949, when Gayle was nearing the end of second grade, the Cummins family moved seven miles across town to 101 Mohawk Street on the west side of Dearborn. Like their old neighborhood, the area was not too ethnically diverse, except for a few Polish and Italian immigrant families. Besides the change in schools for the kids, the family also decided to begin attending a new church in the nearby city of Wayne. First Baptist Church of Wayne would be home for Gayle for the next four decades.

It is difficult to overstate the importance of biblical faith in Gayle's upbringing. Gayle's father, Emery, developed a passion for Bible study at an early age. Emery's father was a Detroit policeman with precious little time to prepare to teach his

Sunday school class, so Emery was often tasked with doing the research and preparation. Emery also grew up singing in church alongside his dad and three brothers, as well as jazzing up old hymns with his trombone.

Emery was also a gifted preacher, with a special love for Old Testament narratives and prophecy. Many Sunday evenings were spent filling pulpits of area churches, in which Emery would lead the worship and preach the sermon. Gayle chuckled as she said, "He would be there the whole evening, you know." Oftentimes, his older son Em—Gayle's older brother—would accompany his father on the piano. Em would later recall those church services as some of his fondest childhood memories.

Emery and Georgina always made time to read the Bible and kneel alongside the children to pray, whether at the supper table or just before bedtime. To the Cummins family, the Bible was true and its standards right. Such were the beliefs taught by Emery, both in his itinerant ministry and in his large Sunday school class for young families at First Baptist Wayne. Although drinking, dancing, and going to the movies were forbidden, Gayle confidently said she grew up in a "real happy home." And nothing made Gayle happier than summertime at Maranatha.

Maranatha

Besides working long hours at Ford Motor Company, Emery Cummins bookended his weeks with church on Sunday morning and an informal seminary-type class on Friday evenings. With Gayle and her brothers safely in the care of a babysitter on Friday evenings, Emery and Georgina would dress up and drive into downtown Detroit for Bible class. The class was taught by the medical doctor-turned-pastor and Bible teacher M. R. DeHaan, who founded the Radio Bible Class in Grand Rapids. It was DeHaan who suggested Emery take his family for a week the following summer to Maranatha Bible and Missionary Conference Center on the shores of Lake Michigan, next to the city of Muskegon. Gayle was six months old.

Maranatha's roots go back to 1936, when Dr. Henry Savage, pastor of First Baptist Church of Pontiac, Michigan, used the grounds for a boys' camp. Two years later, Dr. Savage booked the grounds for the whole summer, calling it Maranatha Bible Conference, and bringing aboard a young man named Howard Skinner as manager. Over the next decade, Skinner added several cottages to the property. It was also Skinner who approached Emery in 1951 about buying a cottage high on the dunes overlooking the lake. Although Gayle's first ten summers only included one or two weeks at Maranatha, a cottage of their own meant Georgina and the kids could spend all summer at the conference center. Emery had to work in Dearborn and joined them on the weekends.

With its two-pronged vision as a Bible and missionary conference center, Maranatha made sure people of all ages got plenty of both. Children, youth, and adult services were—and still are—held morning and evening, with at least one evening each week devoted to hearing from a missionary about their ministry. From before she can remember, Gayle memorized Bible verses in the white children's chapel, which was located where the tennis courts are today. According to Gayle, the steepled church was "just like you picture in the storybooks."

Once, when Gayle was in about sixth grade, she memorized Psalm 121 and recited it before the adults in their adult chapel meeting. "That one really stuck out in my mind. It's a short psalm. 'I will lift up mine eyes unto the hills. From whence cometh my help? My help cometh from the Lord.'" Maranatha quickly became a safe haven and refuge. Never a summer went by that the Cummins family did not grow spiritually.

The only downside to a Maranatha summer for Gayle was that it could not last. Eventually summer came to an end, turned to fall, and families reentered the real world outside. After fourteen summers as a Maranatha child, Gayle faced such reality. Like awakening from a dream, Gayle would never quite be the same. And it all started when Gayle's cousin asked her if she'd like to go *cruising*.

CHAPTER 3

Opposites Attract

It was a tense twenty minutes for the two young men, both of whom were nearly the same age. On one side of his living room stood a resolute Buzz, determined that soon he and Gayle would get married and find their own happily ever after. Across from Buzz stood Em, Gayle's older brother, who had recently returned from Wheaton College for Christmas break. Em's plea was simple: "Let my little sis graduate from high school, please, before you guys get married." Twenty minutes later, Em climbed back into his car to drive the 5.9 miles back to his parents' house in Dearborn and tell them his message didn't take.

Upon graduating from Wayne Memorial High School, Buzz found himself on a walking route delivering mail. College was not an option, mostly due to his poor grades. Yet still as popular as ever, Buzz filled his nights and weekends hanging out with friends. While winters in Michigan can be bitterly cold, summers balance them out with sunny, hot days, which Buzz liked to fill with drinking, dancing, playing sports, and chasing girls. One day in the early summer of 1957, Buzz spent his day off with a group of high school buddies playing softball at Camp Dearborn. After playing ball all day, Buzz and company drank their way into the early morning hours, to the tune of Buzz not getting home until close to sunrise, according to his little sister, Janet. Unfortunately, all-day softball earned Buzz severe sunburns and heat blisters, so much so that he could not physically don his mailman uniform and mailbag. The post office fired him for not showing up. Buzz had not kept the US Postal Service motto: "Neither snow nor rain nor heat nor gloom of night stays these couriers from the swift completion of their appointed rounds" ("Postal Service Mission and 'Motto,'" https://about.usps.com/who-we-are/postal-history/mission-motto.pdf).

On the bright side, Buzz soon found a factory job yanking automobile fenders off the assembly line on the afternoon shift. It was backbreaking work. Yet the real pain, at least for Buzz, was that shift drastically cut into his social life.

Cruising

The *Old Farmer's Almanac* reports that in mid-September 1957, the weather in Wayne, Michigan, was warm with little rain. In other words, it was perfect weather for cruising. Teenagers and young adults in the 1950s often spent weekend evenings driving around town, usually with a date or a group of friends, almost aimlessly until one's growling stomach signaled it was time for a bite to eat. Cars filled with these teens and young adults would then congregate at local restaurants. One of the most hopping destinations for cruisers in Wayne was Ray's, a drive-in restaurant where carhop waitresses served fifteen-cent hamburgers and seven-cent soda pops through a car's driver's side window.

While cruising with friends one evening, Buzz waved at the driver of a passing car, whom he knew to be Janet Cummins from high school. Yet Buzz had never before seen the girl in the passenger seat. Deciding instantly to follow Janet's car, Buzz and his friends soon parked in front of the girls' car at a nearby gas station. Janet's sister Judy exited the car to make a phone call, while Janet and her cousin Gayle watched as Buzz slowly walked toward them. Yet instead of approaching Janet on the driver's side, Buzz surprised everyone by walking around to introduce himself to Gayle. "My name is Buzz," he said.

At only fifteen years old, Gayle looked quite mature. In a split second, Gayle decided to use her middle name—Suzanne. Gayle recalled, "I thought that was prettier or something. For a while there I did tell people that when I was meeting them at first. Just the fact that I probably thought I'd never see him again." Buzz asked "Suzanne" if she and her cousins could meet them the following evening at Ray's, although a specific time was not set. "I guess he was planning to be there quite a while," Gayle said with a hint of laughter in her voice.

Gayle spent the night at her cousins' house that evening. The three stayed up late looking through Janet's old yearbook for pictures of Buzz. The next evening, they drove to Ray's to see Buzz Armstrong.

As Gayle tells the story of that evening at the drive-in restaurant, one gets a picture of tons of cars both parked in and circling around the corner lot on Ford Road. Although Buzz dreamed of owning a '57 or '58 Chevy, at that time he had a Ford Fairlane that was aqua and cream two-tone, roughly a year or two old. Janet gave Gayle permission to sit in the parked Ford Fairlane with Buzz, and immediately the two hit it off. Buzz became convinced Gayle was his destiny.

"They Weren't Real Impressed"

Just a few days after that first night at Ray's, Buzz began finding reasons to visit Gayle. He'd often pop in to say hello when Gayle was babysitting in the evenings. Unfortunately, working second shift at the factory severely inhibited such opportunities. For Buzz the only logical course was to quit his job, which he did within three weeks of meeting Gayle. It was a decision that shocked his father, who believed working his way up at a factory was one of the quickest ways to make a good living.

Within a few weeks, the relationship became serious enough that Gayle felt it time to introduce Buzz to her parents. As Gayle described that first meeting,

They weren't real impressed, but they weren't really too worried either at the time. They wanted to know whether he had Christian parents or not. And I didn't know for sure at that time. But I did mention to my folks that they had been church-going people. I didn't know that they kind of stopped when they moved up [to Michigan]. Buzz said he didn't go much.

In other words, Buzz failed to impress Gayle's parents. In Gayle's brother Em's words, their parents believed Buzz was "beneath her." To an extent, this is understandable considering how opposite Buzz and Gayle were. Buzz was from the South (which northerners generally view as less sophisticated), enjoyed a great measure of personal freedom, drank alcohol frequently, worked in a factory, and was nineteen years old. Gayle was the only daughter of a Ford plant manager, a Bible-believing and church-going Christian, an excellent student, and a fifteen-year-old junior in high school. To quote the old cliché, "opposites attract."

It is and has always been a powerful desire for good, moral girls to imagine the cool, rebel guy singling them out as their one and only love interest. Perhaps the girl believes they can change the guy, reforming and saving him from the blazing, fast-lane life he's leading. Doubtless this feeling is real for countless teenage girls. No less so for Gayle Cummins. Yet there seemed simply no way Gayle's parents would affirm the relationship.

As the fall of 1957 waned, Buzz and Gayle debated running away to get married. Gayle's parents were not naïve and knew such plans were in the works. At Christmas time, they sent Gayle's brother Em to plead with Buzz to let Gayle finish high school. Until that encounter, Em had only heard over the phone and in handwritten letters via his parents and brother Rich what was going on. Needless to say, Em had already formed a very strong opinion of how unfit Buzz was for Gayle. As mentioned above, Buzz would not budge.

Saddened and angry, Gayle's father put his foot down. With both parents watching, Gayle called Buzz and voiced the lines her father wanted her to say: they were breaking up. On his end,

Buzz hung up the phone confused and devastated. Nevertheless, Buzz and Gayle continued seeing each other.

"Fit to Be Tied"

Shortly after the breakup call, Buzz and Gayle sped up their timetable for possibly running away together. One night in early January 1958, Buzz told Gayle to be prepared for him to pick her up. Instead, Buzz had car trouble and could not get ahold of Gayle. "Several hours went by. He didn't come. I was kind of fit to be tied," Gayle remembered. So, Gayle took matters into her own hands. After her parents and younger brother, Rich, had gone to bed (with Em having already gone back to Wheaton College), Gayle snuck out the basement door into the night. To her horror, Gayle did not know what to do:

> I just got out to the road and there was a little neighborhood nearby and I tried to decide what to do. I was so worried about everything. So I did go knock on a door. It was safer then. This nice, old couple had me come in and wanted to know what was wrong and let me use their phone. They were just so nice. I had quite a little bit of money in my purse. I called a taxi and I got [to Buzz's house]. Oh, it was just a real rough thing. We just sat up and cried and talked. Then I called my folks at about six in the morning. I tried to catch them before they'd go downstairs. They'd already been down there and knew I was gone.

The result of this unfortunate debacle was Gayle being sent away from Wayne to spend eight days with her father's mother, whom she called Grandma Swingle. (She had earlier remarried a man named George Swingle.)

Looking back, there is no doubt God had his hand on this situation. As bleak as things seemed that January in 1958, probably no other person was more perfect for counseling Gayle and her parents than Grandma Swingle. This caring saint lived with her husband in Napoleon, Michigan, which was near Jackson. In Napoleon, Grandma Swingle could be near her youngest son, David, who was Gayle's father's youngest brother by sixteen years. David pastored a small, Baptist church, which allowed him a degree of status and a voice to which one ought at least to listen. More than that, however, was the fact that Grandma Swingle herself had gotten married as a teenager.

After eight days together, Grandma Swingle was convinced Gayle really was in love with Buzz. Despite Gayle's young age, Grandma Swingle counseled her son to let Gayle and Buzz get married.

The Plan

Upon their return to Dearborn, Gayle's father called together all involved parties for a heart-to-heart conversation. Gayle's parents, Buzz, and Buzz's father, John Armstrong, all gathered in Gayle's parents' living room to discuss how to move forward. Once Emery Cummins indicated that he was willing to let the marriage proceed, John Armstrong suggested the couple get married near Buzz's brother, Jack, who was stationed at Chanute Air Force Base in Rantoul, Illinois, just outside Champagne. Everyone agreed.

In early 1958, Buzz's oldest brother, Glyn, and his wife, Donna, drove Buzz and Gayle to Rantoul, Illinois. Even by today's standards with our interstate highways, it is a long trip. In the living room of a local Baptist minister, whom Gayle remembered as an old but kind and sincere man, the happy, young couple became Mr. and Mrs. Buzz Armstrong. Pomp and circumstance—there were none. Opposites attracted and finally and fully met. Thankfully, they would not be true opposites for long.

CHAPTER 4

Just as I Am

B uzz's mind raced as the congregation of First Baptist Church of Wayne continued singing the invitation hymn, "Just as I Am." Although the hymn only has six choruses, the worship leader decided singing through the whole song several times couldn't hurt. As Buzz and Gayle walked to their car after the service, Buzz sighed, "Whew, that was something! If they would've sung one more chorus, I would've gone forward." Within the hour, Buzz would fall to his knees in repentant prayer.

After getting married in Rantoul, Illinois, Buzz took his sixteen-year-old bride back to his parents' house in Wayne. Buzz's parents refashioned their basement into a small apartment for the newlyweds. "They were just so kind. I just can't tell you how special they were to me," Gayle reminisced. Buzz and Gayle lived there for a few months until they could afford to rent a nearby brick duplex with a yard.

The transition was difficult at first for Gayle, as it is for every new bride. Some nights after Buzz had fallen asleep, Gayle would softly cry because she missed her family, especially her parents. After getting married, Gayle quickly dropped out of high school, at once having a husband and a baby due in October. Buzz found a job at a box factory that paid $65 per week. They had to sell Buzz's Ford Fairlane and purchase an old car built in 1939, for which they only paid $35, but a place of their own was not long in coming.

Another constant of Gayle's life that changed that first year was not being able to spend the summer at Maranatha with her family. Before she got married, Gayle spent every summer at Maranatha. Toward the end of that first summer in 1958, a friend of Gayle's mother, Marj Essenburg, offered to throw Gayle a baby shower with all their Maranatha friends. So Gayle's father drove her to Maranatha for the weekend. Buzz stayed home at their rented duplex in Wayne. Unfortunately, a few Maranatha friends could not come until later in the week, so Gayle and her mother hastily decided to stay a few extra days. As the Cummins' cottage did not possess a telephone at the time, Gayle simply wrote a letter to her husband in Wayne telling him about the change in plans. Buzz was furious. He wrote a reply that Gayle described as "stinging."

Stay Off My Blue Suede Shoes

Whether Buzz did not know what to do with himself without his wife is uncertain, but at some point during these couple of days, he called his parents and told them he was alone. It so happened that Buzz's father, John, was taking the family to the company picnic for the Wayne County General Hospital that evening. Buzz decided to come along. What happened at that picnic is a telling example of the man Gayle had married, as well as the kind of person Buzz would leave behind when he came to a saving faith in Jesus.

As everyone did in those days, Buzz and his family dressed up for social events. The company picnic was no exception. Buzz threw on his favorite pair of dark khaki pants, dress shoes, and a starched, yellow button-up shirt. The yellow dress shirt was a gift from Gayle's brother Em, and Buzz loved the color yellow. Buzz's brother James upped the game by sporting his blue suede shoes.

While standing together waiting to get their drinks, a young guy about Buzz's age kept moving and swaying in such a way that he kept bumping into James. After a few bumps, Buzz had enough. Just as he had done when they were children, Buzz stood up for James. "Hey, you're scuffing up my brother's blue suede shoes!"

The bumper looked amused. "Yeah? What are you going to do about it?"

The challenge was met by a quick jab from Buzz, and the fight was on.

When Gayle arrived home the following day, she was startled to find a crumpled, yellow dress shirt lying on the floor of their bedroom closet. The fight must have eventually involved a number of participants, because Gayle picked up the shirt to find the entire back ripped out. "What happened here?" queried Gayle. Buzz related the story, making sure to emphasize how he was just defending his brother, who probably would have simply gotten his drink, sat down, and brushed off his shoes. All Gayle could say was, "Oh my goodness!" Recollecting this incident, Gayle was not sure if she could have stopped the fight had she been there. Clearly, Elvis was right in warning, "You can do anything, but stay off my blue suede shoes."

Horseshoes

Not long after the picnic brawl, toward the end of summer, Buzz's box factory went on strike. As organized strikers do, laborers were assigned times to carry the picket signs demanding higher wages and better work conditions. When it was someone else's turn to carry signs, the box factory employees passed the time talking and playing all sorts of games. Buzz's favorite diversion was playing horseshoes, and he was unbeatable. All sports came naturally for Buzz, but horseshoes was a cherished game because he had grown up playing it with his father.

Man after man challenged Buzz to a game, always leaving bested but still in good spirits. Eventually a man who was said to have a bit of money bet Buzz he could beat him. All of a sudden, according to Gayle, Buzz was bringing home $14 per day. This means that horseshoes earned Buzz more money than his factory job!

As the strike progressed into September, the birth of Buzz and Gayle's baby loomed near. Between the horseshoe money and a special charity grant in Detroit for out-of-work laborers that Gayle's mother heard about, Gayle and Buzz had enough money to pay for the coming hospital bills. In truly extraordinary fashion, God provided as Gayle gave birth to their first child, Calvin Buford Armstrong II, born on September 25, 1958. Giving birth three weeks before her due date led to some emotional distress for Gayle, having to stay an extra few days in the hospital to ensure the baby's lungs were working properly—a terrifying experience for a young, first-time mother.

A Little Talk with Jesus

Before Gayle's father consented to Buzz marrying his daughter, he asked Buzz to promise him that he would take Gayle to church at First Baptist Wayne every Sunday. Buzz agreed. Some fallout occurred from this decision, such as a few friends of Gayle's parents not speaking to them for a time, thinking they had brought shame on the church. Gayle's father, Emery, voluntarily stepped down from his role as a deacon, believing he had not "managed his own household well" (1 Timothy 3:4).

Nevertheless, Buzz and Gayle attended services every Sunday. For the first time since moving to Michigan over twelve years prior, Buzz heard the gospel preached regularly. The pastor of First Baptist at the time was a man named Norm Vernon. Reverend Vernon, who had in fact roomed with the famous evangelist Billy Graham at Wheaton College, was neither shy about preaching the gospel nor skittish about welcoming Buzz into the church family. In Gayle's words:

> [Buzz] loved that man (Norm)! He, [Uncle] Wayne, and my dad, were all about the same age as the pastor and his wife, Helen. So, they were just a really good influence. It was a little easier for [Buzz] to loosen up and talk to them really in a way because he knew he was still having to work hard in his relationship with my folks.

While Buzz's box factory was on strike, and even after, Gayle's father kindly asked around the church if there were any odd jobs Buzz might undertake to earn some extra money. So Reverend Vernon and his wife always seemed to find something for Buzz to fix or paint. Every time Buzz came to their house, Reverend Vernon carved out time to talk with him. It can easily be assumed that such endearing behavior went a long way in causing Buzz to truly listen to what Reverend Vernon then had to say from the pulpit on Sunday mornings.

One Sunday in October 1958, when Buzz and Gayle's baby was only a few weeks old, Reverend Vernon asked an overseas missionary on furlough to fill in for him in his absence. Neither Buzz nor Gayle would ever forget a memory the missionary shared of a friend. The friend's wife was lying on her death-bed and knew it was time to say goodbye. Looking into her husband's eyes, the wife smiled and thought of heaven. "Honey, I'll meet you at the East Gate," she whispered.

Gayle was unsure how Buzz might react to such a senti-mental illustration. Yet the image stuck in Buzz's mind through the sermon's conclusion. The worship leader then led an invi-tation hymn, meaning a song during which anyone in the congregation could come pray with the pastor if they felt God wanted them to either become a Christian or rededicate their life after having gone astray. The invitation hymn chosen that Sunday morning was "Just as I Am." These are the words Buzz sang that day:

> Just as I am, without one plea,
> But that thy blood was shed for me,
> And that thou bid'st me come to Thee,
> O Lamb of God, I come! I come!
>
> Just as I am, and waiting not
> To rid my soul of one dark blot,
> To Thee whose blood can cleanse each spot
> O Lamb of God, I come! I come!
>
> Just as I am, though tossed about,
> With many a conflict, many a doubt,

Fightings within and fears without,
O Lamb of God, I come! I come!

Just as I am, poor, wretched, blind;
Sight, riches, healing of the mind
Yea, all I need, in Thee to find,
O Lamb of God, I come! I come!

Just as I am, Thou wilt receive,
Wilt welcome, pardon, cleanse, relieve,
Because Thy promise, I believe,
O Lamb of God, I come! I come!

Just as I am, Thy love unknown
Hath broken every barrier down;
Now to be Thine, yea, Thine alone,
O Lamb of God, I come! I come!

(Charlotte Elliott, "Just as I Am." Composed by William B.
Bradbury. Originally written in 1938. *The Baptist Hymnal.*
Nashville, TN: Convention Press, 1991. Hymn 307.)

As the congregation sang these choruses over and over, the words of the song and the image of the dying wife bidding her husband to "meet her at the East Gate" burned within Buzz. They sank deep into his soul to the point where Buzz knew that he should, indeed, come to the Lamb of God. He did not have to make himself clean. He could not wash away the "dark blot" on his soul. Buzz knew Jesus was calling him to come. For the first time in his life, Buzz was ready to respond.

Buzz did not go forward to the front of the church to pray that day. As soon as he resolved to do so, the service ended. Gayle had not sensed God working in him. When they got in their car to drive home, Buzz announced he had almost gone forward, letting out a sigh of relief. Gayle was absolutely shocked. As they settled into the car with their tiny baby boy, Gayle contemplated what to say. This scene in the car as they drove back to their duplex is so critical to Buzz's new life direction that it merits quoting Gayle at length:

He knew that that story hit home. Because if that were happening to he and me, he wouldn't be able to say, "I'll meet you there." He had told me that even as a little boy and getting into bed, he was thinking, "If I die now, will I go to heaven?" He was having questions from childhood. And then more so as he was getting into the drinking and the wild life. Coming home, then, he was feeling very guilty for his lifestyle and thinking about what he would have to do to turn it around and be heaven bound. So this was bringing that out.

He said, "I'm glad that's over."

Then I said, "Well, honey, it's really not over because of the Holy Spirit." Then I kind of went into a bit about how the Spirit would be calling him and that he needed to make the decision and not put it off. So we just talked, and for some time we were silent on the way home. Then when we got back to our little duplex, we walked inside. I could really sense that he was so close. I said, "Do you think you're ready, honey? We can just kneel down and do it, you and I together."

He said, "Can we?"

And I said, "Yes." Then I said, "I can just show you what to pray. But you be the one to pray it." We must have gone over those details about being so sincere that he was sorry for his sins and wanted forgiveness. He did pray such a wonderful, spontaneous prayer. I wish I could have written it down.

He just said, "Lord, I need you. I need forgiveness." And then he said, "I accept you as my Savior."

Buzz arose feeling new. Because he was. As the Bible says, "If anyone is in Christ, he is a new creation. The old has passed away; behold, the new has come" (2 Corinthians 5:17 NIV). Buzz made a conscious decision to turn away from his old, sinful life and to follow Jesus. To use theological terms, Buzz repented of his sins and found salvation in Christ.

Buzz was ecstatic. He exclaimed to Gayle, "Let's go to your folks' house and tell them!" As Gayle joyfully recalled, "I don't even think we called them. I think we just went!" After wrapping their son in a blanket and placing him in his car seat, they drove to Gayle's parents' house in Dearborn. Needless to say,

Gayle's parents were elated. Emery thrusted his hand out to shake Buzz's hand, grabbing his shoulder with the other. "I'll never forget the scene," said Gayle. "My mother smiled and murmured, 'Thank the Lord!' It was a joyful day of thanksgiving for sure. A new beginning for us all."

CHAPTER 5

Oh, to Be a Dad!

The head deacon of First Baptist Church of Wayne filed into the Armstrong residence with a serious look on his face. Buzz had been warned in a phone call that a visit was coming. Firmly, this spokesman asked the children to leave the room.

"No," Buzz responded flatly. "This is a family thing. We are a family." No one moved.

The deacon then proceeded to chide Buzz for standing by his eldest child, Calvin (also nicknamed "Buzzie," later "Buzz"), as he moved forward with his divorce. However short-lived and unhappy the marriage had been, the deacon objected on biblical grounds. On this point they were correct; no one contested them. Divorce is prohibited in the Bible, except in the case of adultery or abuse. Yet on asking Buzz not to walk the hard road alongside his son, the deacon was incorrect.

Buzz looked at him and declared, "There is nothing my son could do that would make me stop loving him. Right, wrong, or otherwise, I will always love him."

Even before Buzz and Gayle began seriously dating, Buzz dreamed of fatherhood. Early on, he exclaimed to Gayle, "Oh, to be a dad!" This dream came true fivefold.

Buzz became a father on September 25, 1958. As mentioned in the previous chapter, Buzz and Gayle named their son Calvin Buford Armstrong II. They nicknamed him Buzzie and set about the task of becoming parents, which, as every parent knows, is something for which you never feel truly prepared. Nevertheless, Buzzie lit up their home. A month later, Buzz became a Christian and determined to honor God in his parenting.

For Buzz, becoming a Christian was a serious matter. According to Gayle, Buzz would always dig deeply into anything that interested him. Together they memorized Scripture verses, such as 1 Corinthians 10:13, and the lyrics of old hymns like "Amazing Grace." As Christmas approached, Buzz and Gayle memorized the story of Jesus's birth from Luke 2. Holding hands while praying was a given. After church services, Buzz often quizzed Gayle on not only the facts of biblical stories, which were all new to him, but also their veracity. He wanted to know why she believed these doctrines were true. Gayle remembered those days well: "I really can't remember what the questions were, but he had a lot of them! And he wanted answers. So we would get the Bible out and search for them."

Gayle's father gave Buzz a Bible soon after his conversion, and it would soon show great wear and tear, as demonstrated by the notes that lined the margins of many pages. A second gift from his father-in-law was a hefty *Scofield Bible Concordance*, a reference resource that greatly aided the couple's study. At that time, Buzz and Gayle did not feel comfortable attending Sunday school, most likely due to members' opinions of their marriage's questionable beginning. Thus they learned to study alone.

Slowly, however, the men of First Baptist who were Buzz's age began befriending him. As they began attending Sunday school, Buzz learned that First Baptist was part of a fairly competitive sports league among churches in the Detroit area. It didn't take long before Buzz's basketball and softball prowess, for both fast- and slow-pitch, earned him a starting spot on the church teams, and he began forming lifelong friendships. It was also about that time, in January 1961, that Gayle gave birth to another son, Daran.

Now a family of four, Buzz and Gayle felt it time to seriously consider purchasing a house. Renting as a growing family was not desirable. Unfortunately, Buzz's salary alone could not cut it. Working for an automotive parts company—Solar Machine Products—which was owned by Gayle's father, uncles, and a partner, Buzz was often given the most physically grueling of jobs that no one wanted. For example, Buzz was often assigned to bend down and pull oil-soaked steel chips out from under large machines. Evidently, Gayle's father wanted Buzz to experience working his way up from the bottom. To Buzz, however, the work was backbreaking and dirty. Twice in three years he tried his hand at other jobs, first selling insurance, alongside his brother Glyn, and later doing a stint in Ford's Rouge factory. Each time he ended up returning to his job at Solar. To make matters worse, he was placed on the midnight shift.

About a month after returning from Ford, Buzz hatched a plan to work the day shift and have the evenings free to spend with his family. Buzz told Gayle, "Honey, I want you to call up my boss, Chuck. You tell him that I've gone to the store." Buzz then went to the store, making the predetermined conversation true. As instructed, Gayle pleaded with Chuck, with whom she had spoken on a few occasions, to reassign Buzz to the day shift. Chuck could not refuse the pleas of his employee's wife, relentingly telling Gayle to pass on to Buzz that he would start the next morning.

Side Job

Once he started working the day shift at Solar, Buzz's already positive personality glowed even brighter. "That was such a blessing," Gayle reminisced. Yet the change in schedule did not include a salary increase, and so the Armstrongs continued in their rented house.

One day, Buzz's boss, Chuck, invited Buzz to consider a side job: *deburring*. Since sharp edges often form inside the holes of nuts and along the sides of bolts as they are cut, smoothing each piece can be both painful and monotonous. Chuck realized that car companies paid well for people willing to take on such projects, and he knew Buzz needed some extra cash. Buzz mounted a small washing machine motor to the basement work bench. With an attachment that held the bit to the machine, Buzz would get the machine whirring and rotating, place the nut or bolt next to the bit as it spun around the motor, and then use a handheld deburring tool, called an abrasive, to break off the metal burrs. Several times per week, Buzz came home from work hauling two or three five-gallon drums of such nuts and bolts. Gayle and their two little boys often played in the basement to keep their daddy company.

During the day, in between watching her two young boys and frantically completing household chores, Gayle tried her best each day to deburr a red mixing bowl full of the parts. The completed parts were due at the end of each month. Still, as the monthly deadline approached, Buzz and Gayle always found themselves behind on their quota. As a solution, Buzz and Gayle took an hour-long shift each, alternating all night long, for the two or three nights before the due date. Finally, after two years the side job paid off. Gayle said:

> We spent a lot of time with this little odd job. It was amazing, really. But the Lord blessed us, and we were able to start saving some money until we had enough to buy a house—when we had enough to apply for the mortgage. That's what we were working for and it paid off. Praise the Lord.

Family Man

In 1963 Buzz and Gayle bought a ranch-style house on the north end of Treadwell Street. Within walking distance of First Baptist Church of Wayne, it was an area of town that was beginning to be called Westland. The Armstrongs owned that house with a brick front and large family room for twenty years.

The following October, Buzz and Gayle welcomed their new daughter, Valorie. A little girl in the home brought an entirely new dynamic. Like everything else, Buzz threw himself wholeheartedly into learning how to father a girl. All her life Valorie cherished her dad as the one she knew she could run to in hard times. It was Valorie who would recall how, many years later, Buzz defied the First Baptist deacons and chose to love Buzzie through his divorce. Through tears, Valorie stated, "I remember just thinking, '*Oh my goodness! There is nothing I could do that would ever stop my dad from loving me like that.*' I'll never forget it."

By the time Veronica came along in the summer of 1968, Buzz was busying himself by leading all kinds of activities for the kids. Feeling they had earned enough money from the deburring side job, Buzz started a modest lawn-care business and sometimes brought Gayle, Buzzie, and Daran along. Besides playing third base in softball and leading his team as high scorer in basketball, both through the church league, Buzz also coached his sons, Buzzie and Daran, in the city leagues.

According to both Buzzie and Daran, their dad was a great coach. When asked what he was like as a coach, Buzzie underscored his dad's desire to see players develop: "He had high expectations for people to continue to develop and improve, not just their skills but also to understand the game very well." Daran agreed that their dad helped people understand the game, but also noted Buzz's competitive spirit: "He would do what he had to do to win a game, whether that be in baseball a suicide squeeze play at the end of the game or any kind of trick play."

In addition to coaching, Buzz became involved in a number of church-related activities. He taught a junior high boys' Sunday school class (Gayle also taught a junior high girls' class), took up the offering during services, and around the time Veronica was born, he was elected a deacon. He also enrolled his sons in Boys' Brigade, a Christian alternative to Boy Scouts, and became the equivalent of a troop leader. The Boys' Brigade regularly took camping trips around Michigan.

On one occasion, the Boys' Brigade camped near a lake, so Buzz decided to rent a rowboat and take it out by himself. While in deep water, the boat flipped and Buzz could not right it. Signaling and yelling to his friends on the shore to rescue him, the other men believed for a long time that Buzz was only joking. When they finally did come, Buzz had somehow lost his shoes. Luckily, he did not lose his wallet. Gayle explained what happened next:

He stopped and bought himself a pair of shoes. And I said, "You mean, you walked into the shoe store barefoot?"

And he said, "Well, yeah. What else was I going to do?"

I said, "Well, boy, honey, that was good thinking to get them on the way home."

Life at Home

While many men falsely think verbalizing affection is emasculating, Buzz never shied away from telling his family he loved them. Everyone in the family knew Buzz loved them because he said it multiple times per day. In the words of his oldest child, Buzzie, "Telling us and Mom how much he loved us, that was real natural for him." Warm greetings were also commonplace, as Buzz flashed a glowing smile every time one of his children entered the room.

Buzz was a strict disciplinarian, believing the Bible taught parents to discipline those they love. Once, for example, Buzz hunted Daran down with a switch for going to play baseball at the schoolyard without permission. Discipline was always done in love, though, and all of the children understood that. Brooks, born in 1971 and the youngest of Buzz and Gayle's five children, said it created a "healthy fear" with higher purposes in mind:

> He wasn't just Mr. Joyful all the time, like none of us are. So when something was done wrong and there'd be either a rule broken or a disrespect that was going on, you knew it. We all had a pretty healthy fear of him. But it did come from that he wanted us to grow up and be able to respect him so that we would be able to respect God and follow him and obey him ultimately.

The Armstrongs had a fast-paced schedule, with everyone bustling from activity to activity, yet also taking time to play Monopoly, ask thoughtful questions about one another's lives, and participate in family meetings. Buzz would call a family meeting to discuss issues that affected everyone, such as if another child was on the way, and then close each meeting in prayer. And of course, Buzz lightened the atmosphere wherever he went with his thunderous laughter.

Interestingly, Valorie, Veronica, and Brooks all retain the same memory of Buzz's laughter. At that time, First Baptist Church of Wayne maintained a membership of over five hundred, with Sunday services often hosting six to seven hundred adults. As the children's Sunday school classes concluded, so did the main service. Everyone then connected in the large foyer. Veronica remembered the scene vividly, which occurred every week without fail:

> It was just packed. You could not see a specific person in the sea of it. So I'd come to the edge of [the foyer], and I knew that I needed to find my family and my parents so we could get together to head home to have roast or whatever we were having. So I'd come out and my friends would be with me and I'd stand there and wait and listen. All of a sudden, I'd hear my dad's amazing laughter, with his huge cackle laugh. I'd listen for it and I'd move in that direction. Then I'd get up to him and I could see him with his head rolled back. He'd throw his head back and be doing his huge laugh, his arms wide open and legs spread out.

No matter the season, whether good times or hard, Buzz's laughter was loud, strong, and constant. Veronica summarized, "No matter what, he always had that joy. The joy of the Lord."

Maranatha

One of the most significant parts of Buzz's joyful life was the emphasis placed on summers at Maranatha. According to Daran, and affirmed by the rest of Buzz's five children, Buzz "couldn't wait for summer." Just as his wife, Gayle, could not imagine life without Maranatha summers, that also became the case for Buzz.

About the time Buzzie and Daran were in junior high, a cottage on Lake Harbor Road, just inside the main entrance to Maranatha, came up for sale. With three small bedrooms, a modest kitchen, and a living room with a large window looking out onto the baseball field, the white cottage seemed tight but manageable for a family that loved vacationing at Maranatha.

Not far from the tabernacle, where morning and evening services boasted wonderful speakers, Buzz and Gayle viewed the cottage as an answer to prayer. Up to that point, the family had only ever spent a week or two each summer at Maranatha, with the oldest boys, Buzzie and Daran, perhaps staying an extra week with Gayle's parents in their cottage. All of a sudden, Buzz could see himself and his family taking advantage of the Christian atmosphere and beach for an entire season.

How would Buzz make it worthwhile, since he had to work through the summer? Solar Machine Products, where Buzz was now quality control manager, graciously gave Buzz four weeks of vacation per year. He also worked in sales. If he did the math right, and Chuck and the other bosses obliged, Buzz could take Mondays and Fridays off to spend with his family at Maranatha. This is precisely what happened. From the time school let out in early June until Labor Day in early September, Gayle and the kids stayed permanently at Maranatha. Much like Gayle's father did when Gayle was growing up, Buzz spent as long as he could each weekend at Maranatha before heading back east to Westland. Except Buzz cut it closer than Emery Cummins ever would have felt comfortable doing. Leaving the cottage at 2 a.m. on Tuesday morning, Buzz would arrive at work by 7 a.m., work late, work all day Wednesday and Thursday, then leave directly from work on Thursday, bound for Maranatha. Meanwhile, on Tuesday and Wednesday evenings at 10 p.m., Gayle would hurry down to the Maranatha Lodge to call Buzz using a pay phone, not having a phone or television for many years in the cottage. Summer after summer, Buzz and Gayle sacrificed this way so their family could imbibe the spiritual atmosphere in what Daran called a "Christian's paradise."

As the years went by, Maranatha always remained a constant. It was something that all of the family members looked forward to, each in their own way. As each of the kids reached the ages of fifteen or sixteen, they worked on the conference grounds and found lifelong Christian friends. For Buzz, Maranatha contrasted sharply with the gray realities of bills and shift work. Summers at Maranatha were about more than the pool and beach volleyball; they represented his faith that God was about the business of doing beautiful things in this world. Neither he nor his prayer warrior wife could have imagined how greatly that faith would be tested in the coming years.

CHAPTER 6

Faith through Heartbreak

With no food left in the cupboard, Gayle fell to her knees. The kids had all gone to school and the house was quiet, except for the soft prayer Gayle was lifting up. Since Buzz did not have an income, Gayle begged God for direction. All of a sudden, Gayle heard a knock on the door. Getting up from her knees, she opened the door to find friends from church holding $300. The deacon board decided to give them the deacon fund. As she closed the door, Gayle was overwhelmed at how instantaneous the Lord's response came. "Right while I was still on my knees, the Lord answered."

Sometimes the most exciting and lucrative business opportunities end in disaster. But such realities can only be seen in hindsight. This was certainly the case for Buzz in the early 1980s. Gayle's father and brother invited Buzz to go in with them and buy a used automotive parts supply shop in Ypsilanti.

The purchase would take five years to complete, according to the paperwork. Yet this was not to be. Another partner in the purchase, with whom Buzz had worked and always viewed as honest, began taking part in some "shady" extracurricular activities, to use Gayle's terms. Only about a year into the deal, the company went downhill fast. Somehow funds were diverted, possibly through missing merchandise, that led to missed payments. Missed payments led to the former owner getting the police to change the locks. Lawsuits, phone calls from the IRS, court orders, and finally bankruptcy followed.

Unfortunately, the purchase of the shop occurred just as a major recession hit the US economy, and the automotive industry was one of the hardest hit. While multinational firms like Detroit's big three—Ford, GM, and Chrysler—struggled to keep profits above water, automotive parts suppliers sank rapidly. The big three began promoting in-house manufacturing, leaving small companies like those Buzz worked for to fend for themselves. Quoting her brother Em's sentiments at the time—who by then was a licensed psychologist with a PhD from Michigan State University—Gayle remembers him saying, "A man works all his career for the American dream, only to see it fall apart."

At the time it certainly did feel like the American dream had turned nightmare. Besides the aforementioned troubles with Buzz's career, which affected not only Buzz but also several members of Gayle's family and their families, Buzz and Gayle had taken out a loan for their house and car that was tied to the success of the new business. In almost a breath, it was all gone.

Fortunately, the bank allowed the Armstrongs to remain in their house for a year. This arrangement allowed Valorie to graduate from John Glenn High School in Westland in 1983 before the move. Then, after a shortened summer at Maranatha and before the new school year began in 1984, Buzz moved his family from the house they'd owned for twenty years to a town forty-five miles west called Pinckney.

Fictional Scene: Long Walks

How did Buzz and Gayle make it through those times? The short answer is that their faith in the Lord and in each other only strengthened. Yet to explain this answer involves a series of snapshot memories, simultaneously uplifting and emotional. What follows is a fictional scene that could have occurred at any point during this period of the early 1980s. While this scene is not an actual memory, it is certainly based on family members' real memories. We begin with Buzz and his family finishing dinner at the table.

BUZZ: What a wonderful meal, honey! I just love a good roast on Sunday!

GAYLE (*smiling*): Oh, thank you, honey!

BUZZ: Okay, girls. Your mom and I are going to go out for a walk. Keep an eye out for Brooks. Where is he, anyway?

VERONICA: He said something about shooting hoops out back.

BUZZ: Well, that's okay. We'll be back in a bit. I love you, girls.

VALORIE and VERONICA: Love you too!

Gayle runs out to join Buzz in the front yard. The sound of a basketball bouncing is heard in the background as the couple begins their walk south toward Glenwood Road. They are holding hands. Gayle waits a minute or two before speaking.

GAYLE: The Lord's going to make a way through this, honey, I know.

BUZZ (*sighing*): I hope so. I guess tomorrow I'll have to find the nearest unemployment office and apply. I sure never expected to have to do this.

GAYLE: I know. (*long pause*) Do you think I ought to call some more friends tomorrow? I can ask if they could help us get through this month.

BUZZ: Thank you, honey.

GAYLE: The others said they didn't have much to give, but they could give a little.

BUZZ: Praise the Lord. They are planting a seed, you know, for our family. We will pray God blesses them financially for it.

Buzz's voice trails off for a moment. Gayle waits for Buzz to begin again. The kids' elementary school, Schweitzer Elementary, can be seen up ahead.

BUZZ: It is such a blessing that Daran has that basketball scholarship to Wayne State. He has that rickety old car your brother sold us. Valorie is getting ready to go to Spring Arbor University. Is Buzzie's job at the convenience store going okay?

GAYLE: He says it keeps him busy, which is good. I hate that he has to work there after getting a business degree from Eastern Michigan. I didn't have the heart to tell him the deacon from First Baptist came by this week.

BUZZ: Yes, that's probably for the best. Boy, was I shocked that they told us not to stand by Buzzie through this divorce. It's hard not to feel the judgment from everyone at church. I don't know, maybe we should think about going to another church.

GAYLE (*feeling tears approaching*): Well, I've been at First Baptist my whole life. I wish there was another way. I never dreamed that we would be treated this way. Maybe you're right. What could be worse than going through all this?

BUZZ (*stops and looks at Gayle*): We will be okay, honey. We've got each other. We've got our health. We've got the children who have got their health. God is still good.

Pinckney

In the summer of 1984, Buzz and his family moved into a rented house in Pinckney. Aside from a short stay in nearby Howell, Pinckney was home for the next twelve years. Veronica entered eleventh grade at Pinckney High School. Brooks started seventh grade at Pinckney Middle School. Gayle recalled, "It was neat to start over in a way too. New surroundings. New church." Yet Gayle also admitted being scared at times. Buzz, however, considered it an adventure from the Lord.

Not long after arriving in their rented house, Buzz noticed an automotive parts shop around the corner that looked similar to those he had worked in back in Wayne. As Buzz walked into the shop called Patterson Products, amazingly he recognized the owner from many years prior. The owner and his wife gave Buzz a job in sales. The salary was low but sufficient, provided the family kept a tight budget.

Three months after arriving in Pinckney, the owner of the rented house informed Buzz he was going to lose the house and they needed to move as soon as possible. Sadly, a similar story greeted them for the next several moves. Yet the Armstrongs stayed within the Pinckney school district so Veronica and Brooks could remain in their same schools. Unfortunate also for Buzz, his work life mirrored his ability to find sustainable housing, as Patterson Products went under in four years and Buzz jumped from one job to the next. Nevertheless, both Veronica and Brooks graduated from Pinckney High School. Like their older siblings before them, they then went on to college.

God showed himself faithful though, and everyone counted their blessings. For example, Buzz became a founding elder of a new Presbyterian church plant called Cornerstone in nearby Brighton. The church grew rapidly, and Buzz even helped consecrate the first building by dipping a shovel into the freshly dug dirt. Both Veronica and Brooks also met their spouses, Dave and Kelly, in Pinckney.

Obviously, Brooks was affected the most throughout this period. Being the youngest child, he spent junior high, high school, and community college in Pinckney. When asked about his perception of the time, however, Brooks pointed to his mother and father's faith pulling them through:

> It was really something. Especially knowing what I know now and how hard that would have been, going through something like that. I know how hard that must have been, now being older. But the coolest thing I remember from that is that it wasn't even a blip on the radar when I was young. I couldn't even have known that they were going through it. I do remember the stories and the prayers. They did lean heavy, and my mom's always been a prayer warrior. I remember that. Lots of praying and all that. But the biggest thing I took from that is that I didn't realize anything was going on. Maybe I was a little clueless, but I know it was that they had such a faith that there was nothing that could have impacted them. They knew their priorities. They had their priorities right—God and family. So, it was pretty cool that it didn't impact me like that.

One Last Move

After Brooks graduated from high school and was established at Hope College, Buzz and Gayle decided it was time to move permanently to Maranatha. With all their financial woes of the previous twelve years, it is amazing they were able to keep their summer cottage. This fact alone shows how significant

Maranatha had become to the family. As Buzz slammed the car trunk, started the ignition, and pointed his car west toward Maranatha, he began the last move of his life.

CHAPTER 7

One-of-a-Kind Grand-Dad

On September 26, 1985, Buzz Armstrong assumed a new title: Grand-Dad. This part of the story becomes personal for me, since my birth gave Buzz that title. It is here that I enter the story. I am the first of Buzz Armstrong's grandchildren, the oldest child of Buzzie, who married Karen in 1984 and went on to have a successful business career. I write these words with pride, not in myself but in the endearing legacy my Grand-Dad has passed on to all of us. In my cousin Amara's words, he was a "one-of-a-kind Grand-Dad." If someone were to take the time to enumerate all the children, grandchildren, and great-grandchildren produced from the union of Buzz and Gayle Armstrong, they would find a number that is quickly closing in on one hundred people. Yet even more remarkable than numbers is the fact that all their offspring love Jesus Christ and his church. A full family tree is provided in the appendices.

This chapter is unlike every other chapter in this book because it is a chapter of simple memories. These memories are neither chronological nor exhaustive. Taken together, they paint a vivid picture of how Buzz interacted with those of us who called him Grand-Dad.

Grand-Dad and Grandmama's Maranatha cottage holds a special place in the hearts of their grandchildren. Living in nearby Grand Rapids, April was blessed to spend several overnight visits each year. April would always spend at least one full week at the cottage each summer, plus single-night stays here and there.

April loved these overnight visits with Grand-Dad and Grandmama. She did not, however, love the early morning wake up calls. Often April's mom, Valorie, would drop her off and remind Grand-Dad, "This is her vacation. Let her sleep in if she wants." Yet the excitement of hosting his oldest grand-daughter outweighed sleep, at least in Grand-Dad's mind. April laughingly recalled:

> He could hardly take it! As soon as he was up, he'd be at my door making noise or announcing what Grandmama was making for breakfast that day. He was just so antsy to get going. Once he was awake, the day needed to start. It was just like he was super excited to share it all.

Having grown up in Tennessee, my brother Conner cherished the week or two each year our family spent at Maranatha. Often, Conner would climb onto the porch swing of Grand-Dad's cottage and listen as Grand-Dad spoke about how much he loved life and loved living in Maranatha. Conner remembered several occasions where Grand-Dad talked in typical overstatement about how Michigan was "the greatest place in the world!" Of course, Grand-Dad viewed Maranatha as the best of the best. Grand-Dad's porch swing declaration about Maranatha: "It's got it all!"

For many years, the Armstrong family held large reunions in Big Rapids, Michigan. These were joyous times, where all of Grand-Dad's extended family came together for fun, food, and lots of laughter. As Brock tells it, the reunions also consisted of lots of golf. The oldest of Daran's sons, Brock was the first to accompany his dad, Uncle Brooks, and Grand-Dad onto the golf course.

One year, Brock and his brother Jack, again joined their dad and Grand-Dad for golf. Brock rode in his dad's golf cart. Yet this time, Grand-Dad let six- or seven-year-old Jack drive the golf cart. Brock sniggered as he said, "He drove Grand-Dad right into a pond. I thought that was hilarious. Drove him right into a pond!" For some reason, Grand-Dad still let Jack drive after the incident. Later that day, Jack drove their golf cart through a fence. "Then my dad wouldn't let Jack drive the golf cart after that," Brock concluded.

One of the most fascinating memories to surface from my interviews with my cousins was how impressed they were by Grand-Dad always being happy to see them every time they walked through the door to Grand-Dad's cottage. Everyone remembered the loud greetings and broad grins, as if Grand-Dad had been waiting all day for their visit. Here I quote two of my cousins:

Brayden reflected on his surprise at how Grand-Dad was always excited to see him:

> Whenever I would see him or interact with him, it didn't matter how long it was since the last time I'd seen him, he would just get this big smile on his face. He'd be like, "Come here, handsome boy!" He'd give me this big hug. It didn't matter, he was always just so happy to see me. I was able to relate, because that made me so happy to see him too. It didn't matter if I saw him the day before or if it had been a week before I saw him. Every single time, he was so excited to see me and just talk and be together. It didn't matter how long, even if it was just like that day.

Grace said she will always remember Grand-Dad's ability to make her smile as she entered the cottage:

> One thing that I continue to remember and that makes me feel like he's still around is whenever I'd walk into the cottage and I was in my teen angst and just not very happy or not smiling, he'd say, "Let me see that smile." And as soon as

he said that, you couldn't deny that you wanted to smile. I always think about that whenever I am feeling that way.

Speaking of Grace, she had the unique privilege of living with Grand-Dad and Grandmama at Maranatha longer than any other grandchild. When Grace was in high school, her family moved to Uganda to serve as missionaries for two years. Grace lived two summers at Maranatha, and the second of those years she also spent the fall there in order to take the ACT exam to apply to colleges.

One evening around 9:30 p.m., Grace was sitting with Grand-Dad and Grandmama in the living room of the cottage. Grand-Dad all of a sudden looked over at Grandmama. "Oh, honey, you know what sounds great right now?"

"What?" asked Grandmama.

"An apple pie!"

Laughing, Grace said, "So we started making him an apple pie. And it wasn't done until midnight. He loved it! Grandmama didn't even have a piece of it!"

Grand-Dad believed in the power of prayer. From his earliest days as a new believer, individual and family prayer played a significant role in his spiritual formation. Everyone who shared a meal with Grand-Dad and Grandmama heard him pray personal, specific prayers for family and friends.

When asked how Grand-Dad showed his love for Christ, more than one of my cousins with whom I spoke pointed to his prayer life. Having spent multiple overnight visits at the cottage, April stated that she knew Grand-Dad's faith was real by the way he prayed. According to April, Grand-Dad "prayed like crazy for everyone. Before eating, he'd pray so specifically for each person in his life. That was just really cool to see such examples of when they said they were praying for you, they really were praying for you."

There was no pizza place around Maranatha that Grand-Dad enjoyed more than Mr. Scrib's. I will always remember it as one of the greasiest pizzas I have ever eaten. When I told Grand-Dad that, he laughed deeply and handed me another slice.

Amara remembered dining at Mr. Scrib's Pizza one day with Grandmama and Grand-Dad. "We never really did that," said Amara, referring to dining inside the restaurant instead of ordering delivery. That day, there was a fairly long line of clients waiting at the counter. Grand-Dad and Grandmama were sitting in a booth while Amara stood in line. All of a sudden, Grand-Dad and Grandmama "broke out in a duet." Amara recalled:

> It was just so loud! Thinking about it now, it just warms my heart. But then it was so embarrassing! Then when you think they're going to stop, and they don't, and they're just singing this whole entire song in this restaurant really loud. You're like, "Oh, that's a great one. Uh-huh." You just don't really know what to do! But now just thinking about it makes me smile. Everyone was looking, like, "What is going on?"

Grand-Dad's laugh was contagious, loud and clear with his head thrown back. Much of his days were spent laughing. As mentioned in previous chapters, Grand-Dad's laughter was his identifying trait for many.

Brayden called Grand-Dad's laugh a "big, deep belly laugh where, when he thought something was funny, he'd just go off." Brayden often thinks about his dad Brooks and Grand-Dad retelling a story together and laughing all the way through. Evidently, Grand-Dad liked to stop at roadside produce stands on the way home from work and buy a single tomato to eat on the drive home.

> My dad tells it like it would just be this big, juicy tomato and it would be getting all over his shirt. And he'd just be laughing. They'd both just start laughing so much. That's

exactly like Grand-Dad. He wouldn't care. He just enjoyed those little things. Like a tomato driving home from work. But for some reason, he would just be so into it and enjoy it and wouldn't even realize it would just be getting all over his shirt. That story was great because they'd just both get laughing. Grand-Dad's laugh was the best.

Yet life was not always laughter and sunshine for Grand-Dad and his family, as the previous chapters indicate. Sometimes Grand-Dad's kids and grandkids made life choices they would regret for the rest of their lives. Through it all, Grand-Dad never stopped loving them.

Amara has given me permission to share that her first marriage was "horrible," as she describes it. When Amara finally found the courage to admit this fact to someone, she turned to Grand-Dad. Across the breakfast table at Cracker Barrel, Amara explained that she needed to get out. In Amara's words, "He gave me a huge hug. Pretty much let me cry on his shoulder. He just said, 'There's nothing you could do, even if you stay with [Amara's first husband], I'm going to love you no matter what.'"

Grand-Dad's words and actions, according to Amara, reflected the person and love of Christ. At such a low point in her life, where she said even her faith was "on the brink," Amara felt from Grand-Dad a supernatural, unconditional love.

Conner's words are a fitting conclusion to this chapter on how we grandkids feel about Grand-Dad:

> When I think of a place that's joyful, I think of being in Grand-Dad's presence. I always think of the happiness of being there in the cottage. I remember a professor in seminary saying, "If you're looking for Jesus, one of the best places to go is where there's a lot of laughter. If there's no laughter, that's probably not a place where the Spirit is going to be found." In His presence, there's blessing forevermore. So I think about that. I think about the joy.

CHAPTER 8

Full Quivers

Gayle was confused. Never had she entered a room with her husband inside and not received a warm and loving greeting. "Honey, are you okay?" she asked.

Buzz shrugged, "Oh, sorry, honey. I'm just not feeling myself."

After dinner, Gayle noticed Buzz struggling to squeeze toothpaste on his toothbrush. Gayle first thought he was joking. Then she suspected trouble. Leading him to sit down on their bed, Gayle directed Buzz to place his left hand on his nose. When he could not perform this task, the picture became clear. "Honey, you're having a stroke."

On a bitterly cold January day, Buzz and Gayle Armstrong parked their car outside their Maranatha cottage and began hauling their belongings inside. The year was 1994. The white, summer cottage would forevermore become their permanent home.

The family had never lived at the cottage in the winter. Equipped at that time with only a fireplace in the living room, Buzz and his youngest child, Brooks, spent many hours gathering, splitting, and stacking wood that had either been purchased or donated. Yet the heat from the fireplace only reached so far, and Gayle found that as night came, the cold became unbearable in the adjacent bedrooms, bathroom, and kitchen. "I'd try to hurry and do the dishes before nightfall, because I just wouldn't have been able to be warm enough," Gayle recalled. It was not until a few years later that they could afford to add a furnace.

That first year after the move, Buzz continued drawing a meager check from the insurance company where he worked, which was based in Howell, Michigan. Gayle found work painting and re-wallpapering rooms in other Maranatha cottages. For many months, in Gayle's words, "We just made do."

Help-U-Sell

In late 1994, Buzz received a call from his older sister Clara. The call was actually an offer: Would Buzz like to join her real estate company Help-U-Sell, as they expanded from Big Rapids to Grand Rapids? Smelling a challenge and a much more reliable paycheck, Buzz agreed.

On a good day without much traffic, the drive from Maranatha to Big Rapids takes over an hour. This meant quite a commute for Buzz as he trained to become a licensed real estate agent. Fortunately, Buzz was always a quick learner. He quickly passed his exams.

As anyone who ever started a new business endeavor can attest, the first several months of Buzz trying to open a Help-U-Sell location in Grand Rapids was not easy. Well into 1995, after several more months of barely making ends meet, Gayle found herself in the dentist's office. According to Gayle, that's when the Lord spoke to her: "It seemed like the Lord just gave me the idea of being quiet, sitting in that chair waiting for him. It seemed like he was saying, 'You need to get your license. You could earn more money than wallpapering and painting.'"

Buzz was overjoyed that his life partner would also become his business partner.

After a week-long training, including lessons linking the Emancipation Proclamation to reasons why African Americans ought to have full rights to choose their own properties, Gayle passed her own licensing exams. Gayle still held on to her painting and wallpapering side jobs, but after several months decided to focus solely on real estate. All told, Buzz and Gayle worked together for twenty-two years.

Over these years, many clients and business associates asked in amazement how the couple could work together without any marital friction. The reason was twofold. First, Buzz and Gayle played off each other's skill sets. Buzz loved sales and spending time with people, whether buyers or sellers. Gayle smiled as she said, "He was such a good salesman. Such a winning way with people." For her part, Gayle enjoyed creating and listing profiles and putting ads on the market.

The second reason the business worked was because Buzz and Gayle devoted it to God. Instead of working for profits, buying and selling was always set in ways that made it easier for clients to move forward. Often, such an aim meant Buzz and Gayle would have to chip in some of their business's own money to meet costs. While this was not considered shrewd business by other real estate companies in Grand Rapids, clients began to realize something was attractively different about Help-U-Sell.

It was not long before God opened doors for Buzz and Gayle to share their faith with their clients. "The Lord would lead us to people that were open to hear our testimony," Gayle said. Their winning personalities created lifelong friendships. Life was moving in a positive direction.

Then came a stroke.

The Stroke

A stroke occurs when blood flow from the heart to the brain becomes blocked. Buzz's stroke came in December 1995. It would mark one of the final turning points of his life.

One day as Gayle was painting a room in a nearby Maranatha cottage, Buzz stopped by to tell her he did not feel well and that he had decided to come home early from work in Grand Rapids. Gayle told him that she would be home soon. She then cleaned her brushes, let them soak, and trudged home.

As Gayle walked to the door, she saw Buzz stumble and drop the firewood he was carrying, an odd occurrence for sure-footed

Buzz. Gayle stooped to help Buzz get the firewood in place, settled him into his chair by the fire, and then remembered they did not have food for dinner. Gayle recalled, "I believe by that point his stroke had already started." At the time, however, she had no idea. Gayle made a quick trip to the grocery store as Buzz lightly snoozed in his chair.

When Gayle returned, Buzz did not greet her. At that point, Gayle began to realize something was wrong. After the episode with the toothbrush, and Buzz's inability to perform the simple task of touching his hand to his nose—a test used by paramedics suspecting a stroke—Gayle drove Buzz to the emergency room. Buzz spent four days in the hospital, with Gayle by his side the whole time. Over the next year, blood thinner medicine, therapy, and exercising at a gym in Grand Rapids—at which Buzz's nephew, David (Mike) Abela, gifted him a membership—led to only minor, lingering effects. The only lasting change seemed to be that Buzz became cold quicker. Nevertheless, Buzz just curled up in his chair with a warm blanket and a smile.

Back to Work

Following his stroke and subsequent recovery, Buzz was itching to get back to work. As Help-U-Sell's reputation became known in the Grand Rapids area, Buzz and Gayle found that sales were picking up. Sales provided them the ability to pay their personal and company bills on time and brought more opportunities for blessing their children and grandchildren financially.

Buzz and Gayle's office was located in Grand Rapids, as was the home of their daughter Valorie. By that point, Valorie and her husband, Scott, had already given Buzz several grandchildren. Some of Buzz and Gayle's greatest memories from their years selling real estate involved taking Valorie and her kids, all homeschooled at the time, out for lunch at restaurants such as Cracker Barrel. Sometimes Veronica would also bring her kids from Lowell, a city due east of Grand Rapids. Gayle remembered:

We'd just be able to treat the kids and pay the bill. That was such a blessing to us! We'd been struggling for several years before that, after we'd lost that little screw machine shop, back when we lived in Westland. So we had been kind of under a shadow of all that. Just making ends meet for so long. This was really our chance to treat the kids.

Closing a sale on a house not only meant extra money, but it also gave Buzz and Gayle further opportunities to witness to their clients-turned-friends of the faithfulness of God. Taking a cue from a scene she'd seen in the Christmas movie *It's a Wonderful Life,* in which the wife of main character George Bailey also assists in the closing of the sale of a new home, Gayle created *blessing baskets.* Each basket cost about $30. Within the baskets were bread, salt, and "wine," which was typically represented by grape juice. The blessing, adapted from *It's a Wonderful Life,* read, "Bread so this house may never know hunger. Salt so life may always have flavor. And wine so love, joy, and peace may remain with you forever." Gayle would also handwrite a note reminding the family she was praying for them. Many of these families stayed in touch with Buzz and Gayle.

Downturns

In 2007, Buzz's health took another downturn. An irregular heartbeat worried the doctors in Muskegon, not to mention Buzz's family. Daran called his longtime friend Dr. Tony Colucci, who ran the emergency room at Henry Ford Macomb Hospital in Detroit. Tony advised Daran to bring his dad in right away. Reluctantly, Buzz and Gayle packed their bags for what they thought would be a one or two-night stay. The heart specialists at Ford Macomb felt otherwise. After initial testing, Buzz had surgery to input a defibrillator and pacemaker, both of which were inserted via the left side of his upper torso.

A few days after surgery, an alarmed Tony called Daran, saying, "Daran, you better get up here and take care of your 'kids.'"

"What do you mean?" Daran asked.

"Well your mom and dad have their things packed on the bed. They just told me this morning they're going home! We can't release him. It would be too dangerous!"

Daran rushed to the hospital and convinced his parents to stay. Finally, on the twelfth day of their hospital stay in Detroit, Tony signed the release papers. Gayle remembered the scene well: "All the way down the hall, you would've just been amazed, Grand-Dad started singing, 'Let's just praise the Lord! Praise the Lord! Let's lift our hearts to heaven! Praise the Lord!'" Buzz sang his way through the hall, down the elevator, and into his car in the parking lot.

Nine years went by with Buzz's pacemaker causing his heart to work beautifully. Then on Halloween 2016, Buzz's kidneys failed. Since the kidneys purify blood, Buzz needed dialysis fast. For the next eighteen months, Buzz spent four hours, three days per week at the nearby medical center in Muskegon for dialysis treatment. For most of that time, a port just above Buzz's collar bone, on the right side of his neck, pumped blood in and out of a dialysis machine, cleaning his blood of toxins and excess liquid.

While the dialysis machine was hooked up to his neck, Buzz was fine. He could still do crossword puzzles with his right hand and use the television remote to watch sports. Staff and other patients even reported to Gayle that sometimes Buzz would loudly sing some of his favorite songs. Only when the Muskegon doctors decided to change to his right arm did the trouble start. Four hours without the use of his right hand became unbearable for Buzz. He began to loath dialysis days.

Buzz spent most of February 2018 in the hospital, as his health seemed to grow even worse. A state-of-the-art surgery, which the Muskegon doctors were reluctant to attempt until all three of Buzz's sons pleaded with them (Brooks and Daran in person and Buzzie on the phone), further opened a heart valve by placing in a stint. This surgery gave Buzz another six weeks to live. It was also the surgery out of which Buzz had just come when my wife Jessica and I arrived with our baby daughter from the Grand Rapids airport. As I mentioned in the

Introduction of this book, it is the only time my daughter met my Grand-Dad.

"You Can Go, Honey"

Over the weekend of March 24, 2018, nearly all of the Armstrong family gathered around Buzz in his Maranatha cottage one last time. Regrettably, my family and I were in North Carolina that day. I am told that it was a bittersweet time for everyone.

My brother Conner and his family stayed on at Maranatha for most of the following week to help. At one point, Conner took his truck to Grand Rapids and brought back a hospital bed for Buzz to sleep in, with the hope that it might make him more comfortable. "I think he slept in it one night," Conner said softly. Unfortunately, Conner, an army chaplain, had to leave for home on Wednesday to report for reserve duty. His wife, Amy, begged him to let them stay one more day. They both knew they could not.

On Wednesday evening, March 28, Gayle admitted to Veronica's husband, Dave, that it was time to call 911 for an ambulance. Buzz had by that point missed his Monday and Wednesday dialysis treatments, plus Gayle was worried that he would not stay in the hospital bed. The doctors gave Buzz some morphine dabbed on a sponge, causing Buzz to fall into a relaxed sleep. Gayle slept in a chair beside the bed.

After a fitful Thursday night in a second room, this time containing two beds, the Friday morning sun shone bright through the hospital windows. On the US calendar, March 30, 2018, was Good Friday. It is called such because Jesus Christ was crucified for the sins of the world on a Friday, two thousand years before the one on which Buzz and Gayle awoke in the Muskegon hospital. As light poured in, so did the heat from the furnace. Try as they might, neither Gayle nor the hospital staff could turn down or turn off the heat. "I had never been so warm!" Gayle said.

Between trying to keep breathing amid the heat and readying herself in the bathroom, Gayle was praying God would not take her husband until she could be at his side. From time to time, Buzz became agitated and needed a bit more morphine. Valorie and Veronica called and told their mom they were on their way.

When she felt sufficiently presentable, Gayle settled in next to Buzz's left side. Rubbing his hand and shoulder, Gayle remembered how her own father as he was dying had appreciated knowing she would be alright if he died. She also quoted a psalm:

> Then the Lord brought [to mind] that passage about the quiver, that God had told us years before that "happy is the man that has his quiver full; his children gathered around his table will be his protection." I said, "So, see, honey? You've done it for us. We've got these children with their families and all of our grandchildren. Even great-grandchildren now. So they are my protection. I'll be okay. You can go, honey." And it just seemed that, at the time I finished telling him about that, he just must have decided, yes, he could go home to be with the Lord.

As soon as Gayle finished saying these words from Psalm 127, Buzz perked up. What happened next is astonishing:

> It seemed like right then he kind of perked right up and woke up a little out of that deep sleep. He just seemed to open his eyes and lean forward. I think his bed was propped up too. And he said, "Oh! Oh! Oh!" Three loud ohs. It was just like, there is the Lord! Or his angels. Whatever he could see.

According to Gayle, the tone of Buzz's voice as he cried "oh, oh, oh" was exactly the same as Buzz had uttered so many times when one of his sons had cracked a homerun in a baseball game. "Then he was just gone," Gayle said.

Moments later, a nurse walked in, having most likely overheard the scene. Gayle noted that the time of death was 10:25 a.m. A few minutes after, Valorie and Veronica hustled into the room. Gayle will always be thankful, however, that the Lord answered her prayers to be beside Buzz. They had a beautiful, sixty-year marriage, and she was beside him to the end.

Conclusion

A thousand diamonds glittered across Lake Michigan. The only sound that could be heard on that early morning was that of my bare feet crunching sand. It was late September 2014. My wife and I had come to Maranatha to visit my Grand-Dad and Grandmama. As I ran along the water's edge, a romantic picture filled my mind as I remembered that Uncle Brooks used to do this same thing as he trained for basketball in the off-season.

I had no destination in mind. I just wanted to run and watch the sun come up over the water. Finally, as I turned around to run back toward my waiting shoes, and eventually my still-sleeping wife, a shot of pain from the sides of my feet caused me to wince. The pain grew, but it was not overpowering. When I finally stopped to put my socks and shoes on, I saw blisters lining the bottoms and sides of my feet. As I slowly hobbled back to Brooks' and Kelly's cottage where we were staying, which sits just across the road from Grand-Dad and Grandmama's cottage, I took stock of the situation. If I had known the effect running on unfamiliar ground would have on me, would I have still opened the door and gone down to the beach?

Writing this biography has been much like running on the Maranatha beach that day. Charmed by the romantic idea of writing the story of a man whom I idolized as the saintly patriarch of our Armstrong family, I did not realize several things.

I did not realize the emotion that would arise in family members as I interviewed them about memories that were often painful. I did not realize the scars that have long since faded—scars I have now uncovered. I did not realize how living with my Grand-Dad in my mind this last year would spill over into my own family conversation, so much so that my four-year-old daughter now regularly asks me, "Can you tell me another story about Grand-Dad?" But I also did not realize how I would become so immersed in this project that I would dream of my Grand-Dad and burn to finish telling his story.

In the end, I did not realize how *human* he was. The scars and the hardship, the good and the bad, merely show that our heroes sometimes fall. This is because they are not Jesus. Like us, they are sinners. The only thing truly heroic about our heroes is the parts of them that look and act like Jesus. In this biography, I have tried to show that Buzz Armstrong, my Grand-Dad, grew to look a lot like Jesus.

At the end of his life, he was pointing us all to Jesus, not to himself. Perhaps that is Grand-Dad's most heroic legacy of all. Meeting Jesus completely transformed his life. He made sure then that his family and friends also had the opportunity to experience such transformation. Of course, never once does Jesus promise his followers it will be a cushy, easy life.

Knowing what I know now about the ups and downs of Grand-Dad's life, as well as the toll digging up old memories would take on me, would I have still started the journey? Would I have still gone down to the beach? Without a doubt, yes. I am a better man because I did.

Epilogue

A Legacy Full and Genuine: Grand-Dad's Memorial Sermon

Delivered by Cameron Armstrong
Shores Community Church
Norton Shores, Michigan
April 9, 2018

To begin, I just want to say how incredibly honored I am to be able to stand and testify to the life of my Grand-Dad. Thank you for allowing me the privilege to stand and speak today. Oh, how I loved him! From the age of twenty until his last breath, Grand-Dad lived his life with a laser focus on the One he now sees face-to-face: his Lord and Savior, Jesus Christ. Never was his faith in question by anyone who knew him, and that legacy literally reverberates from the shores of Maranatha to the ends of the earth.

Grand-Dad was a family man. He desperately loved his wife, his five children, his twenty-six grandchildren, and his sixteen great-grandchildren. Even the word *love* seems too soft for the heart-wrenching, hurricane-like affection Grand-Dad showered on all of us. From the youngest great-grandchild to the oldest of his children, Grand-Dad always carved out time to speak to us and pray daily for us by name. And obviously, looking around at the many people here, Grand-Dad's family extends far beyond biological ties. Ever kind to friends, neighbors, and strangers, we all remember how the family cottage on Lake Harbor Road was always packed beyond fire-code capacity with men, women, and children who absolutely adored Grand-Dad and his magnetic personality.

Along with everyone else here, I always knew that no matter where God took me, I'd always have a welcome place beside my Grand-Dad. "I love you, ol' handsome boy," he'd say, as he'd plop a big wet kiss on my cheek. In my younger years I'd try to dodge that kiss, always unsuccessfully. Then we'd sit on the cottage's porch swing rocking away as he'd listen to my boyish ramblings that, if I could go back and analyze them now, probably sounded so outrageous and disconnected.

I often return in my thoughts to that porch swing. Maybe I'm an eight-year-old kid again sucking on a piece of watermelon Grandmama picked up that morning from Meijer. My legs dangle back and forth. It's summertime at Maranatha, with a promise that my dad and Grand-Dad will take my brother and me to the beach soon if we're good. We might even swing by the Sweet Shop.

Maybe I'm sixteen and telling Grand-Dad how tough it really is entering a new high school. "You have no idea!" I'd insist. Soon, though, he'd have me throwing back my head in laughter, just like him. The world always seemed lighter and brighter after those talks.

Or maybe I'm twenty-six and newly married. My Grand-Dad laughs his long, hearty laugh as he sees my eyes light up when my bride, Jessica, walks through the creaky door to sit next to me.

I'll never outgrow that porch swing.

For in my mind, on that swing sits a man with a heart as wide as Lake Michigan. Buford Armstrong, my Grand-Dad, lived and loved well for eighty years. It is hard to underestimate that kind of legacy. How many lives were touched by his life? How many people brought into God's kingdom because Grand-Dad first said yes to Jesus? Countless!

In preparation for this message, I asked Grand-Dad's five children—my dad, Cal (or Buzzie); Uncle Daran; Aunt Valorie;

Aunt Veronica; and Uncle Brooks—if they remembered some of Grand-Dad's favorite verses and hymns. Here are their responses:

DAD (BUZZIE): "I remember him referring to John 1:1 often: 'In the beginning was the Word, and the Word was with God and the Word was God. He was in the beginning with God.' My dad also really loved many of the proverbs about wisdom. As for songs, one of my earlier memories is of him singing a gospel song that I think is called, 'Have a Little Talk with Jesus.'"

I was able to track down this song. Here are some of the words, which are very fitting:

> Now let us have a little talk with Jesus
> Let us tell Him all about our troubles
> He will hear our faintest cry and we will answer by and by
> Now when you feel a little prayer wheel turning
> You'll know a little fire is burning
> You will find a little talk with Jesus makes it right
>
> (Cleavant Derricks, "Have a Little Talk with Jesus."
> Originally composed in 1937. Quoted in *The Golden Age of Gospel* by Horace Clarence Boyer [Chicago, IL: University of Illinois Press, 2000], 151.)

DARAN: He always loved "Up from the Grave He Arose" and "How Great Thou Art."

> Up from the grave he arose
> With a mighty triumph o'er his foes;
> He arose a victor from the dark domain
> And he lives forever, with his saints to reign
> He arose! He arose! Hallelujah! Christ arose!
>
> (Robert Lowry, "Up from the Grave He Arose" ["Low in the Grave He Lay"], originally composed in 1874, *The Baptist Hymnal* [Nashville, TN: Convention Press, 1991], number 160.)

VALORIE: I remember my dad singing "Ring the Bells at Christmas" and teaching me that song. Also "Heavenly Sunlight." And at Easter we sang "Up from the Grave He Arose" over and over. My dad memorized a lot of Scripture as a new believer, and he told me how amazing that was. I have many sweet memories of my dad singing old love songs to my mom. I used to ask him to sing "The House of Blue Lights" (which I loved to hear him do), "Sixteen Candles," a bunch of Sam Cooke, the Platters, and The Silhouettes. In our home we really only listened to fifties music.

VERONICA: My dad loved Isaiah 40:31 that says we will soar on wings like eagles, run and not grow weary, walk and not grow faint. Grand-Dad loved that verse because he was looking forward to having his new heavenly body and being in heaven with Jesus. Also Psalm 139. He was so thankful that the Lord knew him before he was born in the womb and protected him before he became a Christian during his wild, dangerous teenage years. He feels the Lord protected him until he brought Grand-Dad to himself when he met Grandmama. He loved the hymns "What a Friend We Have in Jesus" and "Heavenly Sunlight" and "Rock of Ages," and that one was sung at his dad's funeral, and your Great Grandpa Armstrong often sang that when Grand-Dad was a little boy. I also love thinking about Sunday mornings at First Baptist Church in Wayne when I was a little girl; I would walk into the sanctuary, wait to hear my dad's big laugh, and then I'd know I was safe. Grand-Dad always said that that was the most wonderful time of his life.

BROOKS: Isaiah 40:31 comes to mind first for me. He loved the image of the eagle. As for music, he loved old hymns, especially "Amazing Grace" (he would say he was a wretch before he met Grandmama and through her he came to know the Lord) and "How Great Thou Art." He loved music and was always singing oldies to the kids—"Calendar Girl," "My Girl," "What a Wonderful World" by Sam Cooke, so many to name. He would sing "Zippity Do Da," the cattle song, or "I'm a Lonesome Polecat" from *Seven Brides for Seven Brothers*. He'd always put in your name—whomever he was singing to—to any song, and I thought he made up the song "Pretty Blue Eyes" just for me when I was a kid. He loved to read Buford *The Little Big Horn*. All of these and many more but mostly I will miss his laugh and how much he loved life and all the simple things like spring and the color yellow, mornings and going to breakfast, and just telling stories and being with his family.

It is right and good to remember Grand-Dad like this. It is right and good because his is a life worth remembering, through smiles and laughter as well as through tears and sorrow. And we know that whenever God calls any of his saints home that their death is precious to him. "Precious in the sight of the Lord is the death of his saints," wrote the psalmist in Psalm 116:15 (KJV). Grand-Dad is not here physically anymore, but we are not unaware of where he is. In the letter to the Thessalonians, the apostle Paul wrote:

> Brothers and sisters, we do not want you to be uninformed about those who sleep in death, so that you do not grieve like the rest of mankind, who have no hope. For we believe that Jesus died and rose again, and so we believe that God will bring with Jesus those who have fallen asleep in him. (1 Thessalonians 4:13–14 NIV)

So it is okay to grieve. It is okay to cry. It is okay to sit and think of Grand-Dad and weep at his death, because by weeping we testify that death isn't how things should be. There is an end coming even to death, and the Bible says that death itself is conquered by the sacrificial atonement of Jesus on the cross. Death has lost its ultimate sting. "We do not grieve like the rest of mankind, who have no hope." Grand-Dad knew and lived and prayed and sang and proclaimed that hope all of his days.

I'll never forget visiting him in mid-February at the hospital. Fresh out of surgery, I expected just to watch him sleep. Instead he lucidly, and miraculously, asked my wife and me about our lives and about our baby and later remarkably led all four of us who were in the room in prayer from his hospital bed! Surely, Grand-Dad loved Jesus! If I could pull back the curtain of this world and we could see him now, I think he'd say something like this, "Don't worry, loved ones. I am dancing and laughing with Jesus, my forever Lord. My bones are strong and my strength is back. I'm home." I also think Grand-Dad would look each one of us in the eye and say, "Don't miss this chance to know my Savior. Repent and believe the gospel. It's really all about Jesus today." And, of course, the three words we've all heard thousands of times, "I love you."

Finally, I think Grand-Dad might fall silent for a moment, smile that big grin we all adore, the grin that says, "See you soon, son/daughter, grandson/granddaughter, beautiful wife," and joyfully sing these powerful old words to another favorite hymn:

> Rock of Ages, cleft for me,
> Let me hide myself in Thee;
> Let the water and the blood,
> From Thy wounded side which flowed,
> Be of sin the double cure,
> Save from wrath and make me pure.
>
> While I draw this fleeting breath,
> When my eyes shall close in death,
> When I rise to worlds unknown,
> And behold Thee on Thy throne,
> Rock of Ages, cleft for me,
> Let me hide myself in Thee.
>
> (Augustus M. Toplady, "Rock of Ages, Cleft for Me."
> Originally composed in 1763. *The Baptist Hymnal*.
> Nashville, TN: Convention Press, 1991. Number 342.)

Appendix A

Family Tree

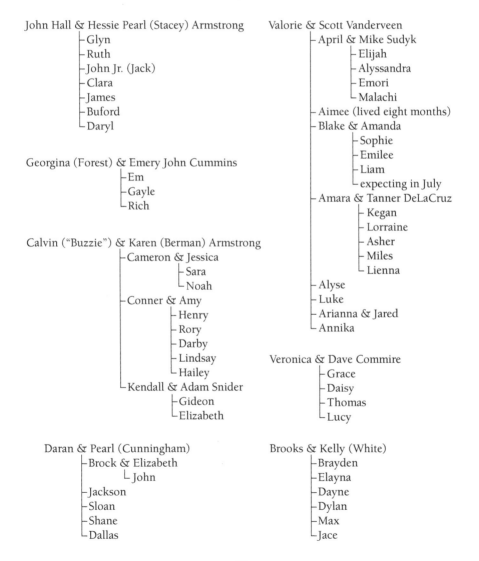

John Hall & Hessie Pearl (Stacey) Armstrong
- Glyn
- Ruth
- John Jr. (Jack)
- Clara
- James
- Buford
- Daryl

Georgina (Forest) & Emery John Cummins
- Em
- Gayle
- Rich

Calvin ("Buzzie") & Karen (Berman) Armstrong
- Cameron & Jessica
  - Sara
  - Noah
- Conner & Amy
  - Henry
  - Rory
  - Darby
  - Lindsay
  - Hailey
- Kendall & Adam Snider
  - Gideon
  - Elizabeth

Daran & Pearl (Cunningham)
- Brock & Elizabeth
  - John
- Jackson
- Sloan
- Shane
- Dallas

Valorie & Scott Vanderveen
- April & Mike Sudyk
  - Elijah
  - Alyssandra
  - Emori
  - Malachi
- Aimee (lived eight months)
- Blake & Amanda
  - Sophie
  - Emilee
  - Liam
  - expecting in July
- Amara & Tanner DeLaCruz
  - Kegan
  - Lorraine
  - Asher
  - Miles
  - Lienna
- Alyse
- Luke
- Arianna & Jared
- Annika

Veronica & Dave Commire
- Grace
- Daisy
- Thomas
- Lucy

Brooks & Kelly (White)
- Brayden
- Elayna
- Dayne
- Dylan
- Max
- Jace

Appendix B

Interview with Chuck Fox
(Grand-Dad's nephew)

December 8, 2020

Note: I include the following interview because Chuck's understanding of my Grand-Dad's life is unique. Chuck knew Grand-Dad both before and after his conversion. Chuck's viewpoint as a non-immediate family member offers a different perspective than that of Grand-Dad's children, yet still affirms the events described in this book.

CAMERON: Well, thank you very much, Chuck, for talking to me about my Grand-Dad today.

CHUCK: Sure. Have they told you the type of teenager that your Grand-Dad was?

CAMERON: Yes, very much a rebel.

CHUCK: Okay. What did they tell you?

CAMERON: They said he was very much a rebel. That he was always kind of doing his own thing. He would be out a lot in the evenings. But he did graduate from high school. So that's good. Then he became a mailman, until he got the factory job. Then he met my Grandmama, of course.

CHUCK: Sure. Well, that's exactly how I pictured him. He had the biker boots and the rolled-up jeans. He had the T-shirt with the cigarettes rolled up under his arm. But even with that type of lifestyle, he still was always around the family. So it's not like he was a rebel and he told my grandparents, "Go fly for it" and "I don't want anything to do with you." He wasn't like that at all. He was still a sweet guy. It was just kind of the guys he hung out with. And the thing, too, that stands out is what a good athlete he was. I'm sure people have told you that. I couldn't believe it. I was a pretty fair basketball player, and so was my brother. And [Buford] had a church team. We used to kid each other all the time, your Grand-Dad and I. He was just wonderful. He would tell me about this church basketball team and how they could probably beat my brother and I and our friends that played in a rec league. I would tell him, "Oh, it's a church league. You probably play against the blind kids." Stuff like that. And he would say something to me. So we finally ended up playing. I couldn't believe how good your Grand-Dad was.

CAMERON: Really?

CHUCK: Yeah. For a guy who didn't have coaching. See, that's the thing. All the brothers, all of his brothers, were really good athletes. Except Uncle Glyn, the oldest. I don't think he played many sports. Of the brothers, Uncle Glyn was the fighter. I remember as a kid, they had a party. Every summer they had a big, giant blowout. Hundreds of people. They all worked at the mental institute. A lot of the family members at one point worked there.

CAMERON: Eloise?

CHUCK: Eloise, correct. As we were leaving as a family, I was probably seven or eight, there was a big to-do as we were leaving. A big fight. My dad got out of the car to see what's going on. When he came back, he said, "Yeah, Buf (Buford) was flirting with some girl and all the brothers got into it." I asked my dad, "Well, aren't you going to go help?" He said, "Nah, they don't need any help." They were doing pretty well. But Glyn was the fighter and Uncle Jack was a world-class tennis player.

CAMERON: Really?

CHUCK: Yeah, he was. Now, again, they all grew up on the farm. Buf was younger—your Grand-Dad. But all the older ones, their whole lives were on the farm. And to think that they were that natural [athletically]. Uncle Jack, he was the armed forces champion in Germany.

CAMERON: Seriously?

CHUCK: Yeah. He played against all the four different branches— Army, Navy, Air Force, and Marines. They also had the best in Europe, and he played against the number six player in the world and beat him. And this is a guy that had no training. I played tennis with Jack for years and years, and it was amazing how good he was. Anytime we'd go anywhere and there was nobody out, there'd be pickup games people would play. No one could compete with him.

Then Uncle Jim (James) played great golf. He started on the varsity basketball team as a tenth grader at Wayne High School. He also worked full-time at Ford. He would get out of school and he'd go to the factory and work his eight hours in the factory. Then he'd sleep and go back to school. But he could play softball and basketball. He was really good. He was a really good golfer. And my mom, she played basketball at her high school in Tennessee. So, it was amazing considering how I don't think your great grandpa and grandma ever played sports. Growing up in Tennessee, I don't think they did that.

My grandpa, your great grandpa, he used to wrestle. He was like the toughest guy in a whole section of Tennessee. They used to wrestle in the gravel. He was a big, tough guy. Sweet as can be to me. But you could just see, anytime he was around people, everybody respected him. He had the final say on things. Jim worked full-time in high school, like I told you, so he had more money than anybody around, and he always bought really nice clothes. He bought like silk shirts and suits. So, he dressed really nice for a guy that was living in Wayne. So, he goes away in the Navy, and your Grand-Dad wore all his clothes and tore up all his shoes. Jim told me that story. He probably told me that story about twenty times. He says, "I come back from the Navy, I go in my closet, and all my stuff was messed up! All my shoes were scuffed up!" He had all these suits and he goes, "Buf just tore 'em all up." So, he laughed about it. Here he goes away in the Navy and Buf, your Grand-Dad, is left with all these amazing clothes!

But when he met your Grandmama, he did a 180! I saw the transition. I was probably twelve years old—eleven or twelve. He just totally changed! He was so in love with her. It was amazing! He dressed different. All of a sudden. He just said, "I'm going to dedicate myself to her." It was pretty amazing. The thing that really impressed me was when he worked for your Grandmama's dad, which is your great grandpa. He owned a business. I can't remember exactly what it was, but they were a manufacturing company. They made something like rivets or something?

CAMERON: Screws.

CHUCK: He had pails of these in his house, in his basement. Your Grand-Dad did. And his business went under. Your Grand-Dad, when he found out they were just going to have to shut the business up, he remortgaged his house so he could pay the employees and try to keep things going. It turned out they had to close up anyways, like six months later. But he actually remortgaged his home just so the people could get their pay. Which is really, you know, what great character!

CAMERON: Yeah, absolutely. So, you mentioned that you saw the total 180 transformation. That's really kind of the narrative that I'm going for in this biography of him. Just how his life changed after he met my Grandmama and met Christ and became a Christian. Do you have any specific memories of interacting with him after that happened?

CHUCK: Well, he wasn't shy about why he did it. He would always talk to me about how important Jesus was. He would constantly say, "You know, Chuck, we're lucky that we have what we have, because I found God." The rest of our family wasn't real religious. My mom went to church and took our family. But most of them didn't really follow much in religion. Uncle Buf would never push it. But we'd have get-togethers and he'd tell everybody we should stop and pray before we have dinner or lunch. He told me how important it was to go. I went to a Baptist church. It was kind of like, with the Catholic church you're christened. He was telling me how important that was. So I went to our church and he showed up. I only mentioned that, "Yeah, in like two weeks, I'm going to go to our church. It's in the evening." I knew that would make him happy. Sure enough, he was there.

Then when my brother passed away ten years ago—actually it was probably ten years ago within a couple days of today—Uncle Buf came to the funeral. It was up north Michigan. On the way back, I called him. I asked him what he thought about people that wanted to be cremated, because that's what my nieces and nephews decided. He thought that was fine and no different. We talked about a couple things. Then he goes, "Well, Chuck, just like when you were twelve years old and I saw you at the church." And I went, "How do you remember that, Uncle Buf?" I said, "You know, that was fifty years ago." He goes, "Hey, stuff like that was very important to me." He remembered exactly when he met me at the Baptist church down from where I lived.

So it's almost hard to explain the look on his face and how things changed when he met your Grandmama. It was like he was, I don't want to sound hokey here, but like he was touched by an angel. He like, all of a sudden, just felt so comfortable smiling all the time. He was a happy guy, but not like this. He just had this glow about him when he was with your Grandmama. Yeah, she was definitely a lifesaver for him. No question.

The other thing I was going to mention with the brothers and them, they were all so close. Every Sunday, from the time I was a child until I was a young adult, everybody met at my grandma's in Wayne. Everybody would show up. She had this little tiny house and she cooked every Sunday. But every single person in the family showed up. They made an effort to always be there. So we had a very close family, which was great memories for me.

CAMERON: Yeah, that's great. Not many people do that anymore.

CHUCK: Yeah, unfortunately, I know. I try to do that. I'm lucky, I've got two daughters and two nieces that we raised as our own. Three of them are within ten minutes of us. We make a point of getting together all the time. We're pretty fortunate. So anyway, all the things I think about Buf was how happy he was, how your Grandmama saved him, and the changes. I remember talking to him about what happened to this friend and this friend and this friend. He said, "Oh, I don't have anything to do with them anymore." So, he really got himself on a good path immediately. And this wasn't something that took years. I'm talking a month. I'm talking immediately. He just said, "I'm dedicated to her and this is what I'm going to do." I don't think that happens a whole lot!

CAMERON: Thank you so much for your time, Chuck!

Appendix C

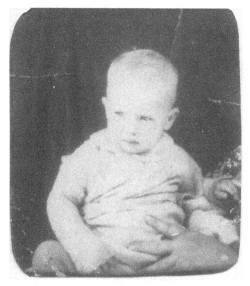

Calvin Buford Armstrong at six months old (1938)

L to R: James Armstrong, Buford (Buzz) Armstrong,
A family friend (c. 1956)

Buford (Buzz) Armstrong's Graduation Photo (1956)

The Cummins family. Back Row L to R: Emery (Em), Georgina,
Emery; Front Row L to R: Richard, Gayle (1953)

The Armstrong family.
Back Row L to R: Calvin (Buzzie), Buford (Buzz), Gayle;
Front Row L to R: Daran, Valorie, Veronica, Brooks (1974)

L to R: Glyn, Donna (Glyn's wife), Buford (Buzz), Dorreen (Jack's wife), John Jr. (Jack) (1978)

Buford (Buzz) in the driveway of their Maranatha cottage (1982)

Buford (Buzz) and Gayle (1990)

Buford (Buzz) and Gayle at Lake Michigan (c. 1990)

L to R: John Jr. (Jack), Clara, Buford (Buzz) (1990)

Visiting Gilley Hill Methodist Church in Hollow Springs,
Tennessee. L to R: Brooks, Buford (Buzz), Kendall (held by Buzz),
Calvin (Buzzie), Cameron, Conner (1992)

Buford (Buzz) (2001)

A Final Word from Gayle Armstrong

I was asked by my grandson Cameron to add a few final words to his Grand-Dad's story. What do I think my husband, Buzz (Buford), would like you to take away from the story of his life? I think he would want me to be candid, knowing times are even tougher now than in the fifties and sixties. Once Buzz turned his life over to Christ and asked for forgiveness of his sins, there was another step that God, through his Holy Spirit, showed Buzz in the months to follow. This was a difficult thing for him to grasp. How could he even begin to walk the path of a Christian husband and father? It was really much harder than one would think. I couldn't do it for him! There were times when Buzz fell from the path God had for him. The Lord doesn't bully us into doing what he wants. He allows us free choice.

So, picking up as Buzz learned to do, seeking forgiveness from God and those he hurt, he would learn from each mistake and try again.

Learning how to pray for your husband or wife, being patient, forgiving, and loving them through their mistakes is crucial! I'm sure many were praying for us. These included Maranatha friends of my parents, First Baptist Church of Wayne, our dear Reverend Vernon, loved ones and other friends—just so many people.

Only God can help you and the one you love to persevere through these struggles. We only need to take our vows seriously! I know there are many who have tried and have prayed fervently to save their marriages to no avail. This is a heartbreak! I cannot even begin to imagine the scope of the deep pain and wounds this would cause those dear ones. Bless their hearts!

Those who have the chance to save their marriages need to keep trying. Buzz and I would tell them the Lord did it for us. Our children benefited, and our lives were so rich, so blessed by our Lord. I know someday in glory, we will never be able to praise our God and Savior, Jesus Christ, enough. He saved us and blessed us with one another. I thank God for our wonderful parents and our family.

We thank God for each of our children and their spouses. What a gift from the Lord that they all love and know Jesus. God gave us precious grandchildren and continues to bless us with our little great-grandchildren.

The verse is important to us about God blessing the man and the woman who put God first and see their children like arrows in their quiver, gathering around their table. They are our protection in our old age.

Each of us, no matter how many children we have or if we are married or single, are blessed abundantly when we put our trust in the Lord. "Thou will show me the path of life: in Thy presence is fullness of joy; at Thy right hand there are pleasures forevermore" (Psalm 16:11 KJV).

I know Buzz would add, and found this to be true, in surrender to him on the path—the narrow path of the cross.

For God's glory,

Gayle Armstrong

ORDER INFORMATION

To order additional copies of this book, please visit
www.redemption-press.com.
Also available on Amazon.com and BarnesandNoble.com
or by calling toll-free 1-844-2REDEEM.

CPSIA information can be obtained
at www.ICGtesting.com
Printed in the USA
LVHW040747080621
689671LV00004B/272

9 781646 453924